The Best of Teacher's Helper *Phonics* Level II

Our favorite reproducibles from the 1984–1997 issues
of *Teacher's Helper*® magazine

Editor in Chief
Margaret Michel

Editor
Susan Hohbach Walker

Contributing Editor
Patricia Staino

Copy Editors
Lynn Bemer Coble
Jennifer Rudisill
Debbie Shoffner
Gina Sutphin

Artists
Pam Crane
Jennifer Bennett
Teresa R. Davidson
Susan Hodnett
Rebecca Saunders
Charlene Shidisky
Barry Slate

Cover Artist
Jim Counts

Typographer
Lynette Maxwell

www.themailbox.com

©1998 by THE EDUCATION CENTER, INC.
All rights reserved.
ISBN10 #1-56234-203-7 • ISBN13 #978-156234-203-6

Manufactured in the United States
10 9 8 7 6 5

Table Of Contents

About This Book

The Best Of Teacher's Helper® *Phonics—Level II* is a collection of the best phonics-related reproducibles published in *Teacher's Helper®* from 1984 to 1997. It is designed to provide an extensive collection of phonics skills in a ready-to-use reproducible format.

Although each reproducible is designed with skill-specific programming, you may find that some pages are too difficult or too easy for your students. To adjust the skill level on a reproducible, white-out the programming and write in your own problems and new directions with a black, fine-tip marker. You may also change problems or directions by masking type with white paper and making a photocopy for duplication.

"Soup-er" Shoppers

Cindy buys soup that begins with the **soft sound** of *c*.
Cathy buys soup that begins with the **hard sound** of *c*.
Write the soup names on the correct lists.

Cathy's List

Cindy's List

cabin   coast

cement   cow   center

cup   cotton   cider   cell

cake   celery   coffee   cent   cab

ceiling   carrot   cedar   color   cinder   city

Bonus Box: You have been asked to develop a new kind of soup by Quackers Soup Company. On the back of this sheet, write the name of your new soup; then write five or more ingredients that will be in the soup.

©1998 The Education Center, Inc. • *Best Of Teacher's Helper® • Phonics II* • TEC931

Follow-Up Activities

— Have students write complete sentences, using a word from each list in every sentence.
— Have students rewrite Cindy's and Cathy's lists in ABC order.

Background For The Teacher
Soup

Everyone knows that chicken soup helps the common cold. And most cooks know that soup is nutritious and economical. But here are some surprising facts about this popular meal.

The earliest evidence of soup-making is dated 6000 B.C.: archaeologists surmise that hippopotamus bones were the primary ingredient in a one-pot soup! In 300 B.C. Esau lost his birthright (inheritance) when his brother Jacob served their father a bowl of soup, assumed to be a red-lentil pottage. Variations of "Esau's Pottage" still exist throughout the Middle East today. "Sop," the medieval ancestor of soup (A.D. 500–1450), described a meal of dried bread in meat drippings. French Onion Soup originated in 1750 when King Louis XV of France mixed onions, butter, and champagne together.

Though people still make their own soup, soup-making is a huge industry. Campbell Soup Company first marketed beefsteak tomato soup in 1895. Two years later, an employee of the company discovered the process for making condensed soup, bringing about a less expensive canned soup. Today the Campbell Soup Company dominates the soup industry, distributing its products in nearly every country. Soup continues to take innumerable forms, as the industry introduces new products to meet the changing demands of its consumers. Low-sodium soups, soups containing dietary fiber, and microwavable instant soups are a few of the more recent developments of the soup industry.

Extension Activities

— Play a class game of tic-tac-toe to review consonant sounds. Label one construction-paper square with each consonant sound to be reviewed (soft c, hard g, qu, etc.). Place squares in a container and draw a tic-tac-toe grid on the chalkboard. Divide the class into teams of X and O. Taking turns, students draw squares from the container, give their word choices, and return the squares to the container. Each correct response earns a play on the grid. The game ends when one team wins by scoring across, down, or diagonally. (Increase the number of squares on the grid to lengthen the game.)

— Brainstorm a class list of words that have a particular consonant sound; then challenge students to use the list to create silly soup recipes like the one below. Encourage students to share their recipes, or use student recipes for daily handwriting practice.

Soup de "/k/"
Cook cabbage, cake, candy, cocoa, corn, and cactus juice in a covered pot for two hours, stirring occasionally with a comb. Serve with a carton of carrot drink.

— Bring in the new year with a celebration of National Soup Month (January 1–31). Enlarge, color, and cut out a soup bowl pattern. Mount on a bulletin board titled "'Quazy' About Soup!" Have students bring in the labels from their favorite soups and copy the soup names onto index cards. Display the cards around the bulletin board. Post a daily or weekly free-time activity to be done with the soup names during the month of January. (Possible activities include: Choose five soup names to write in ABC order, write the soup names with a long e vowel sound, find three soup names that have the hard sound of c, scramble the letters of six soup names and give them to a friend to unscramble, etc.)

Answer Key
(Order of answers will vary.)

Cindy's List	Cathy's List
cement	cabin
center	coast
cider	cow
cell	cup
celery	cotton
cent	cake
ceiling	coffee
cedar	cab
cinder	carrot
city	color

Name _____

The Talk Of The Castle

Read the words on the bricks.
Decide if each word has a hard-*c* or a soft-*c* sound.
Cut and glue each brick to the correct tower.

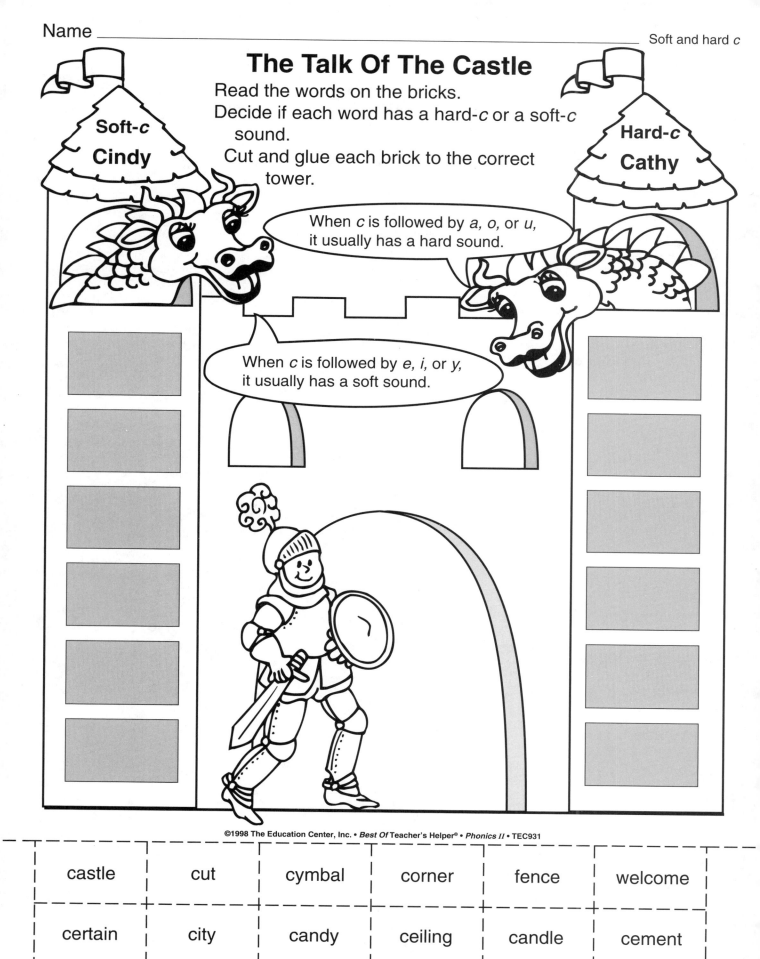

Soft-*c*
Cindy

Hard-*c*
Cathy

When *c* is followed by *a*, *o*, or *u*, it usually has a hard sound.

When *c* is followed by *e*, *i*, or *y*, it usually has a soft sound.

| castle | cut | cymbal | corner | fence | welcome |
| certain | city | candy | ceiling | candle | cement |

Answer Key

Soft-*c* words
certain
city
cymbal
ceiling
fence
cement

Hard-*c* words
castle
cut
candy
corner
candle
welcome

Make "Cents" With Mr. Lincoln

Cut out the pennies below.
Paste over words with *c* as in *cent*.

1¢ car

1¢ cage

1¢ circus

1¢ candy

1¢ coat

1¢ cow

1¢ city

1¢ cereal

1¢ center

1¢ cork

1¢ cell

1¢ celery

Answer Key

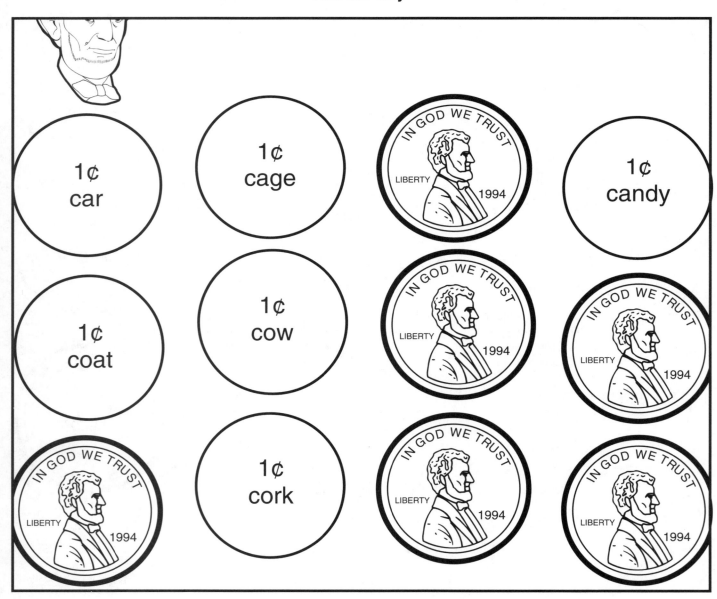

A Hot Challenge

Read the words.
Decide if each word has a hard-*g* or a soft-*g* sound.
Write each word on the correct dragon.

gym

digit

ginger

goose

giant

engine

dragon

gerbil

game

guess

gather

good

gum

orange

When *g* is followed by *a*, *o*, or *u*, it usually has a hard sound.

When *g* is followed by *e*, *i*, or *y*, it usually has a soft sound.

Hard-*g* Gary

1. _____
2. _____
3. _____
4. _____
5. _____
6. _____
7. _____

Soft-*g* George

1. _____
2. _____
3. _____
4. _____
5. _____
6. _____
7. _____

Bonus Box: Choose a book from your desk. Look for hard- and soft-*g* words in the book. Write the words on the back of this sheet.

©1998 The Education Center, Inc. • *Best Of Teacher's Helper® • Phonics II* • TEC931

11

Answer Key

Soft-*g* words
giant
ginger
gym
digit
gerbil
engine
orange

Hard-*g* words
goose
dragon
guess
game
good
gather
gum

Name_____

A Quick Cure

Read the words.
Color the soup bowls.

Get Well Soon!

gem	goose	gum
gentle	giraffe	garlic
goat	gave	gelatin
garden	ginger	golf
game	gerbil	giant
gym	gobble	give
gas	gate	gypsy

Variations

— White-out and reprogram the directions to instruct students to color the three soup bowls on a shelf green if the words are in ABC order and orange if they are not.

— Use the words as a word bank for creative-writing stories entitled "A Quick Cure."

Answer Key

Clean And Green!

Fill in the blanks with **ee** or **ea.**
Then write each word in a sentence on the back of this sheet.

1. fr __ __

2. p __ __ ch

3. wh __ __ l

4. dr __ __ m

5. b __ __ st

6. ch __ __ se

7. sl __ __ p

8. kn __ __

9. b __ __ m

10. __ __ st

11. qu __ __ n

12. t __ __ ch

13. bl __ __ d

14. scr __ __ m

15. s __ __ d

Variation

Reprogram the bars of soap with math facts, missing blend or diphthong words, or root words and prefixes to match.

Answer Key

Fill in the blanks with **ee** or **ea.**
Then write each word in a sentence on the back of this sheet.

1. fr **e e**

2. p **e a** ch

3. wh **e e** l

4. dr **e a** m

5. b **e a** st

6. ch **e e** se

7. sl **e e** p

8. kn **e e**

9. b **e a** m

10. **e a** st

11. qu **e e** n

12. t **e a** ch

13. bl **e e** d

14. scr **e a** m

15. s **e e** d

1, 2, 3, Jump!

Write the correct word on each cloud.
Cross out each word as you use it.

steam

tea

3 three

tree

cheese

seal

bee

feet

seal   three

tree   bee   tea

steam   leaf   cheese   feet

©1998 The Education Center, Inc. • *Best Of* Teacher's Helper® • *Phonics II* • TEC931

steam

tea

3 three

tree

cheese

seal

bee

feet

leaf

seal   three

tree   bee   tea

steam   leaf   cheese   feet

What A Pair!

Circle the correct vowel pair. Write the word for each picture.

ai ee oa	ea ai oa	ee ai oa	ee oa ai
ai ea oa	ee oa ai	oa ai ee	ai ee oa
oa ee ai	oa ea ai	ee ai ui	oa ai ee

Choose 2 picture words above.
Write about these things on the back.

Answer Key

oa	**ai**	**oa**	**ee**
toast	snail	goat	three

ea	**ai**	**ee**	**ee**
seal	mail	feet	bee

oa	**ea**	**ai**	**ee**
soap	leaf	sail	sheep

Sunflower Circles

Write **ay** or **ai** to make a word.
Cut and glue to match the picture and word.

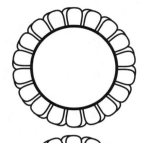
cr _____ on

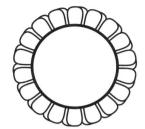
tr _____ n

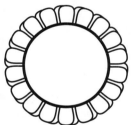
m _____ l

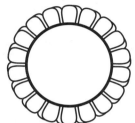
sn _____ l

cr _____
tr _____

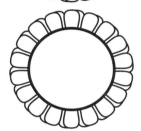
spr _____

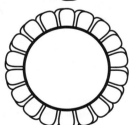
ch _____ n

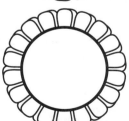
r _____ n

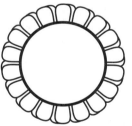
pl _____

t _____ l

A New Skateboard

Read the story.
Circle the words with the same vowel sound you hear in <u>boil</u>.

Boy, is Freddy happy! He has been saving his coins to buy a new toy. Today he bought a new skateboard. He is ready to join his friends.

Freddy will follow the safety rules. He will always wear a helmet and pads. That way a fall can't spoil his fun. He will never ride if his wheels make a funny noise. Freddy will make it a point to keep his skateboard clean. He knows not to use oil on the wheels.

Freddy knows he might fall off his board. He will only wear clothes that can get soiled. Freddy knows he will enjoy his new skateboard. He can't wait to feel the joy of his first ride. We can be proud of Freddy. He has made some great choices.

Choose a circled word to answer each clue.
Write it on the line.

1. the opposite of girl _____

2. great happiness _____

3. a loud sound _____

4. money _____

5. the end of a sharp pencil _____

6. dirty _____

7. to have fun _____

8. goes in a car engine _____

9. rhymes with oil and soil _____

10. a plaything _____

11. rhymes with voices _____

12. to become a member of a group _____

Follow-Up Activities

— Have students create their own sentences or stories using the circled words on the page.

— Have students alphabetize the circled words on the page.

— Have students brainstorm additional words containing the vowel diphthong *oi* or *oy*.

Extension Activities

— Students will skate through vowel practice with skateboard poke-and-say cards. Duplicate several copies of the pattern (see page 38) onto heavy construction paper. Cut out the patterns and punch holes. Program the card fronts with words, replacing the vowel sounds with blanks. Above each hole write a vowel choice. Program the card backs by circling the hole of the correct answer. Laminate the cards for durability. Students poke a pencil through the hole of their choice, say the word, and then turn the card over to check.

— Challenge your students to create sentences using words that contain a selected vowel sound and the words *a, an,* or *the* if needed. Then have students illustrate their vowel sentences. Example sentences: *The* grey ape skates away. It is *a* big singing pig!

— Reinforce auditory discrimination of long and short vowel sounds with this signal game. Students listen to the word called by the teacher, then signal: thumbs up—short vowel sound, thumbs down—long vowel sound. Or give each student two skateboard cutouts (see page 38) to color-code: blue = long, red = short. Students hold up the appropriate cutouts for each word called.

Answer Key

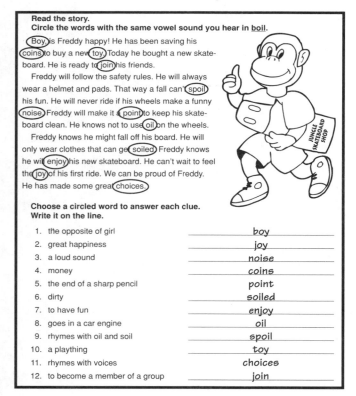

Read the story.
Circle the words with the same vowel sound you hear in boil.

Boy, is Freddy happy! He has been saving his coins to buy a new toy. Today he bought a new skateboard. He is ready to join his friends.

Freddy will follow the safety rules. He will always wear a helmet and pads. That way a fall can't spoil his fun. He will never ride if his wheels make a funny noise. Freddy will make it a point to keep his skateboard clean. He knows not to use oil on the wheels.

Freddy knows he might fall off his board. He will only wear clothes that can get soiled. Freddy knows he will enjoy his new skateboard. He can't wait to feel the joy of his first ride. We can be proud of Freddy. He has made some great choices.

Choose a circled word to answer each clue.
Write it on the line.

1.	the opposite of girl	boy
2.	great happiness	joy
3.	a loud sound	noise
4.	money	coins
5.	the end of a sharp pencil	point
6.	dirty	soiled
7.	to have fun	enjoy
8.	goes in a car engine	oil
9.	rhymes with oil and soil	spoil
10.	a plaything	toy
11.	rhymes with voices	choices
12.	to become a member of a group	join

FRONT

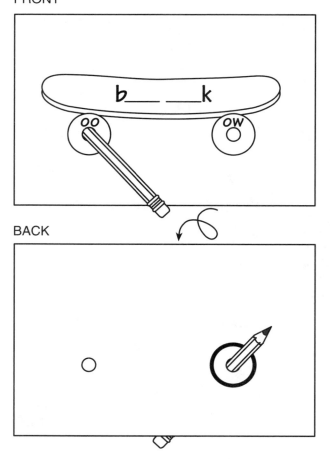

b___ ___k

oo

ow

BACK

Reef Swimmers

Mark the circle beside the correct spelling.
Write the word.

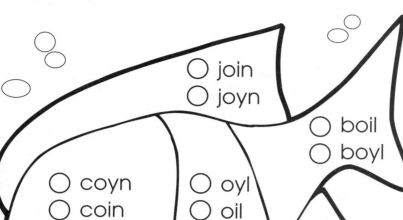

○ join
○ joyn

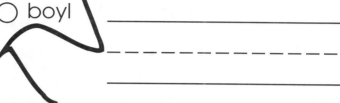
○ toy
○ toi

○ boil
○ boyl

○ coyn
○ coin

○ oyl
○ oil

Write about a snorkeling trip. Use some of the words that you wrote.

○ oink
○ oynk

○ boi
○ boy

○ joy
○ joi

_____

_____

_____

_____

_____

_____

_____

_____

_____

_____

_____

_____

Name _____

Tropical Threesome

Mark the circle beside the correct spelling.
Write the word.

○ auto
○ awto

○ saw
○ sau

○ raw
○ rau
○ paw
○ pau

Write a fishy story. Use some of the words that you wrote.

○ caught
○ cawght

○ daun
○ dawn

○ law
○ lau

○ claw
○ clau

Name _____

Fancy Footwork

Read the word on each sneaker.
If the **oo** sounds like **boot,** draw in a **red** sock.
If the **oo** sounds like **book,** draw in a **blue** sock.
Then choose four of either the red or the blue sock words.
Use them to write a fitness paragraph on your own paper.

 school

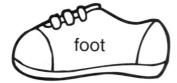 foot

 pool

 too

 good

 shoot

 look

 room

 hoop

 boost

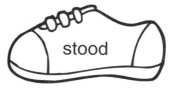 stood

 cookies

 hood

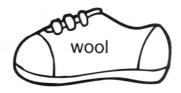 wool

 food

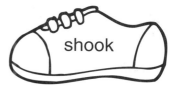 shook

Background For The Teacher

Physical fitness has become a national pastime. In addition to improving physical health, many people exercise for social interaction, personal satisfaction, relaxation, and fun.

Despite the increased interest in health spas, diets, sports equipment, and clothing, the overall fitness of our population is declining. Children who develop healthy lifestyles early may reap the benefits in later life. Encourage students to eat healthful diets and continue daily exercise.

Extension Activities

— Visit a local health spa or fitness center.

— On a chart, compare calories used in various activities such as sitting, walking, running, swimming, bicycling, or jumping rope.

— Have children select a sport to investigate. Discuss training, special equipment, score-keeping, safety measures and rules. Then attend a local athletic event or competition as a group.

— Set aside a time each day to exercise to favorite music. Set class goals for miles jogged around the school track.

— Make a class videotape of a daily workout.

— Have each child choose a famous athlete to write about. Compare amateurs versus professionals.

— Have children collect newspaper and magazine articles for a sports bulletin board. Mount the pictures of famous athletes or favorite team symbols.

Answer Key

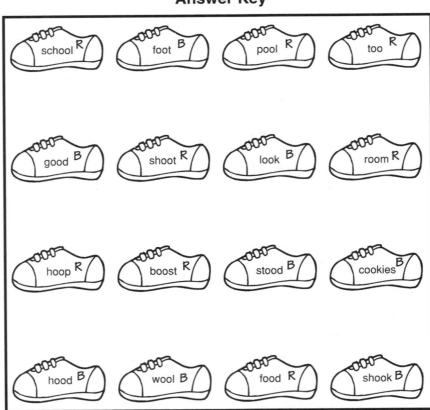

Name _____

Shoot The Moon!

Say each word.
Listen for the vowel sound.
Color the stars.

Color Code:
oo as in **zoo**—yellow
oo as in **book**—orange

goose

good

soon

shook

tooth

boot

moon

food

school

wood

foot

proof

cook

brook

hook

Bonus Box: On the back of this sheet, write the name of the sport you most enjoy. Write a sentence telling why you enjoy it so much; then draw a picture of yourself practicing this sport.

Follow-Up Activities

— Have students create sentences or stories using words
    containing the vowel digraph *oo*.
— Have students brainstorm additional words containing the
    vowel digraph *oo*, then categorize them by sound.

Answer Key

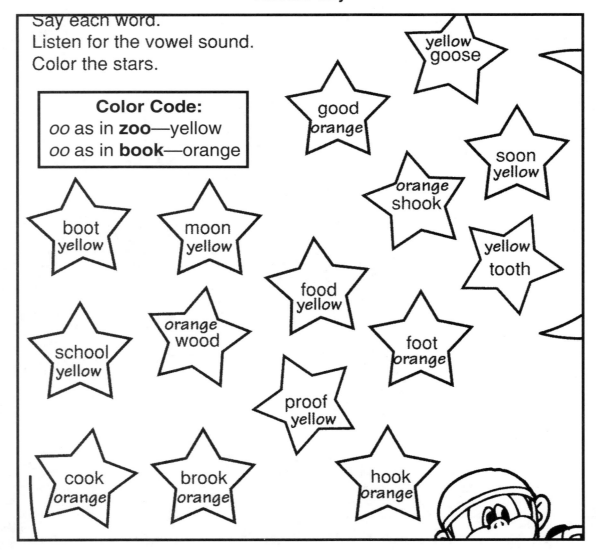

Say each word.
Listen for the vowel sound.
Color the stars.

Color Code:
oo as in **zoo**—yellow
oo as in **book**—orange

yellow goose

good orange

soon yellow

orange shook

boot yellow

moon yellow

yellow tooth

food yellow

school yellow

orange wood

foot orange

proof yellow

cook orange

brook orange

hook orange

Name _____

Santa's Mistake

Fill in each blank with a word from below.
Color the Christmas balls as you use the words.

It was _____ on the day before Christmas. Santa's elves did not

know what to do. Santa had to look at the toys very _____. Did the

toy trains make a loud _____? Did the toy _____ go

cock-a-doodle-do? Were there two _____ on the feet of the toy

fireman? Did the toy _____ lay an egg when you pushed her head?

Only Santa could check all the toys. But where was Santa?

One elf decided to sweep the _____. He looked in the closet

where the _____ was. There was Santa! He had locked himself in!

Santa felt so _____.

Everyone had to hurry. The _____ was shining in the sky. The

sleigh _____ away. Soon it would land on a _____.

Toys would be given to boys and girls. Christmas had been saved!

room   toot   noon   foolish   moon   rooster

roof   goose   broom   soon   zoomed   boots

Bonus Box: On the back of this sheet, draw a picture of Santa's workbench. Put something on the bench that you would like Santa to bring to you.

Variations

— Have students write the words on the Christmas balls in ABC order.

— Use the first paragraph of the story as a story starter. Have each student finish the story in a different way.

Answer Key

It was _____**noon**_____ on the day before Christmas. Santa's elves did not know what to do. Santa had to look at the toys very _____**soon**_____. Did the toy trains make a loud _____**toot**_____? Did the toy _____**rooster**_____ go cock-a-doodle-do? Were there two _____**boots**_____ on the feet of the toy fireman? Did the toy _____**goose**_____ lay an egg when you pushed her head? Only Santa could check all the toys. But where was Santa?

One elf decided to sweep the _____**room**_____. He looked in the closet where the _____**broom**_____ was. There was Santa! He had locked himself in! Santa felt so _____**foolish**_____.

Everyone had to hurry. The _____**moon**_____ was shining in the sky. The sleigh _____**zoomed**_____ away. Soon it would land on a _____**roof**_____. Toys would be given to boys and girls. Christmas had been saved!

Name _____

Let It Snow!

Write each word on the correct snow pal.
Color each snowflake by the color code.

low

powder

grow

shadow

clown

window

arrow

ow as in **snow**

owl

elbow

towel

cow

ow as in **down**

slow

flower

crowd

yellow

drown

Bonus Box: On the back of this page, draw and color a snow pal.
Write a story about the magical things your snow pal can do.

Extension Activities
Snow

— Your students will find it easy to sing this wintry song to the tune of "Frere Jacques." For even more frosty fun, sing the song in a round.

Winter Snow

Snowflakes swirling.
Snowflakes twirling.
Winter day
On the way.
Winter snow is falling.
Mr. Snowman's calling,
"Come and play;
Come and play."

— Here's a fun and unique way to reinforce your youngsters' coolest behavior. You will need several pairs of laminated mittens. To make each pair, decorate two construction-paper mitten cutouts and label each mitten with one word of a two-word motivational phrase. Laminate and cut out the mittens; then punch a hole in the wrist portion of each cutout. Thread and knot one end of a length of colorful cord or heavy yarn in each hole. When a student exhibits exemplary behavior, dangle a pair of mittens around the youngster's neck and give him a hand for a job well done!

— Let it snow! Let it snow! Let it snow! To make these edible snowflakes, each child folds a flour tortilla in half twice. Then, using a pair of sterilized scissors, he cuts a snowflake design from his tortilla just as if it were paper. While the students observe from a safe distance, heat a small amount of oil in an electric frying pan and lightly fry each snowflake. Place the results on paper towels to drain; then let each student sprinkle his creation with powdered sugar. Snow is definitely in the forecast!

Answer Key
(Order of answers will vary.)

ow as in down	*ow* as in snow
drown	yellow
crowd	slow
flower	window
cow	arrow
owl	elbow
powder	low
towel	grow
clown	shadow

Sidewalk Safety

Say each word below.
Listen for the sound of **ow.**
Write the word under the matching sound.

crow
_____
_____
_____
_____
_____

brown
_____
_____
_____
_____
_____

window	crowd	clown	grow	owl
know	flower	yellow	wow	row
show	cow	elbow	crown	

Bonus Box: Think of three safety rules for Freddy to follow while he is skateboarding. Write them on the back of this sheet.

Follow-Up Activities

— Have students brainstorm additional words containing the vowel diphthong *ow* and group them according to the sound the diphthong makes.
— Have students write creative sentences or stories using words containing the vowel diphthong *ow*.

Skateboard Pattern

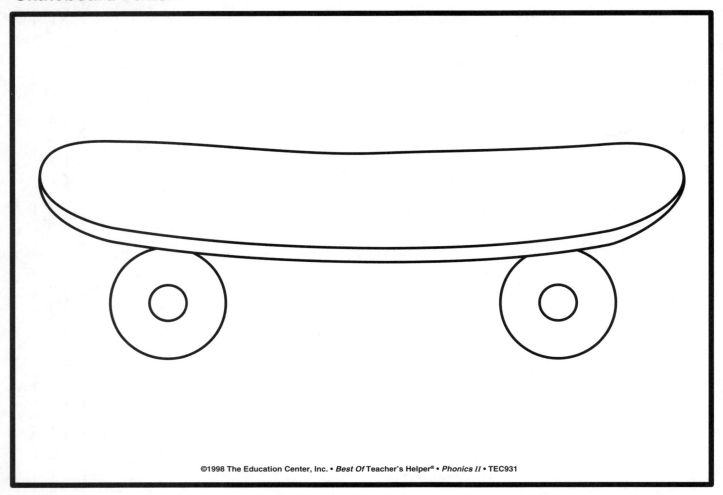

©1998 The Education Center, Inc. • *Best Of* Teacher's Helper® • *Phonics II* • TEC931

See page 24 for ways
to use the skateboard pattern.

Answer Key
(Order of answers may vary.)

br<u>ow</u>n	cr<u>ow</u>
crowd	window
flower	know
cow	show
clown	yellow
wow	elbow
crown	grow
owl	row

Name _____

Seaweed Snacks

Mark the circle beside the correct spelling.
Write the word.

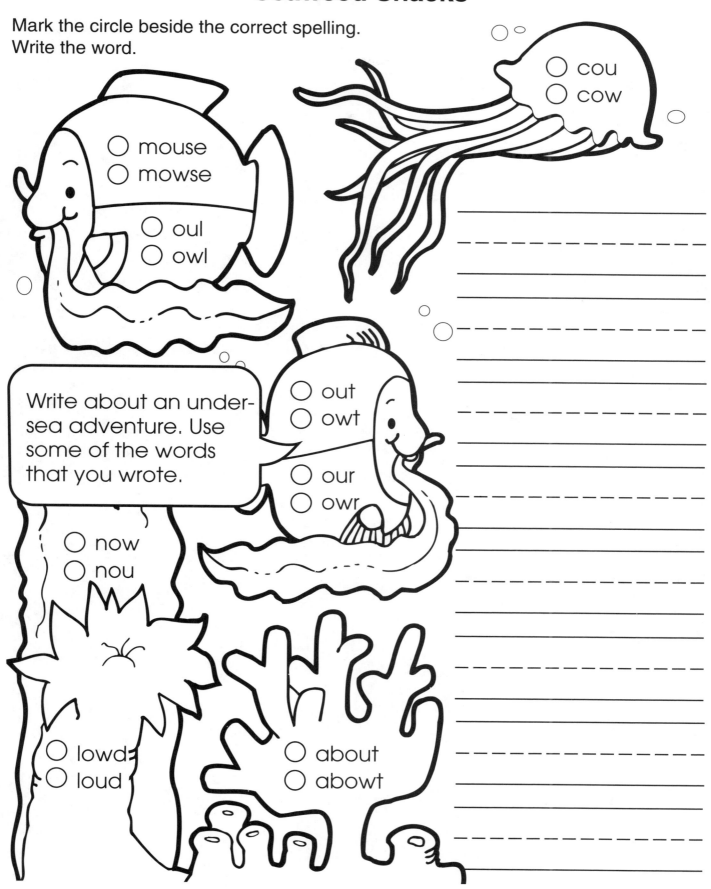

○ cou
○ cow

○ mouse
○ mowse

○ oul
○ owl

○ out
○ owt

○ our
○ owr

Write about an under-sea adventure. Use some of the words that you wrote.

○ now
○ nou

○ lowd
○ loud

○ about
○ abowt

_____

- - - - - - - - - - - - - - - - - -

_____

- - - - - - - - - - - - - - - - - -

_____

- - - - - - - - - - - - - - - - - -

_____

- - - - - - - - - - - - - - - - - -

_____

- - - - - - - - - - - - - - - - - -

_____

- - - - - - - - - - - - - - - - - -

Name _____

Too Loud

Fill in each blank with **ou** or **ow**.
Then circle each word in the puzzle below.

br_____n   cl_____d   h_____

b_____nce   d_____n   m_____ntain

gr_____nd   n_____   c_____

t_____n   ab_____t   sc_____t

h_____se   fr_____n   cl_____n

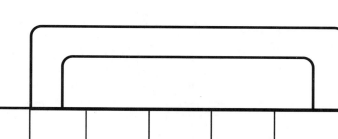

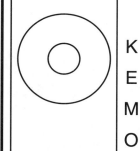

```
K  O  X  E  B  F  R  O  W  N
E  V  C  G  R  O  U  N  D  D
M  S  J  D  O  W  N  M  U  A
O  C  L  O  W  N  I  B  H  B
U  L  A  Q  N  P  T  R  O  B
N  O  W  A  Y  H  O  W  U  O
T  U  O  G  C  B  W  A  S  U
A  D  N  B  O  U  N  C  E  T
I  Z  H  E  W  E  I  I  A  W
N  D  I  U  C  S  C  O  U  T
```

Answer Key

br**OW**n   cl**ou**d   h**OW**

b**ou**nce   d**OW**n   m**ou**ntain

gr**ou**nd   n**OW**   c**OW**

t**OW**n   ab**ou**t   sc**ou**t

h**ou**se   fr**OW**n   cl**OW**n

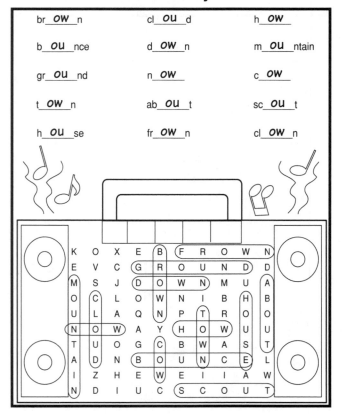

Sunny Sounds

Look at each pair of words.
Color the circle beside the correct spelling.
Cut and glue to match the pictures.

○ crown
○ croun

○ mowse
○ mouse

○ clowd
○ cloud

○ mowth
○ mouth

○ owl
○ oul

○ howse
○ house

○ shower
○ shouer

○ cowch
○ couch

○ cow
○ cou

○ flower
○ flouer

Name _____

Bat Blends

Complete each word using **bl**, **cl**, or **pl**.
Find and circle each word in the puzzle.

____anket

____iff

____ace

____ap

____ast

____end

____ant

____ane

____oset

____aypen

____og

____ind

P	A	G	C	L	O	S	E	T	U
L	C	P	L	A	N	E	H	Y	T
A	B	L	A	N	K	E	T	C	O
C	Y	A	P	R	T	B	N	H	E
E	M	Y	L	Q	C	L	O	G	P
P	C	P	M	T	A	A	T	O	L
B	L	E	N	D	L	S	Y	L	A
S	I	N	E	T	J	T	I	D	N
I	F	R	B	L	I	N	D	C	T
N	F	U	P	R	B	E	I	A	L

Bonus Box: On the back of this sheet, write another word for each blend. Draw a bat around each of your words.

Bat Blends

Complete each word using **bl**, **cl**, or **pl**.
Find and circle each word in the puzzle.

pl_ace

cl_iff

bl_anket

bl_ast

cl_ap

bl_end

pl_ant

pl_ane

cl_oset

pl_aypen

cl_og

bl_ind

P	A	G	C	L	O	S	E	T		U
L	A	C	P	L	A	N	E	H	Y	T
A	C	B	L	A	N	K	E	T	C	O
C	B	Y	L	A	P	R	T	B	N	H
E	Y	M	A	Q	L	C	L	O	G	E
P	M	C	Y	P	M	T	A	A	O	P
B	C	L	P	E	N	D	L	S	T	L
S	I	L	N	E	T	J	T	Y	D	A
I	N	F	R	U	B	L	I	N	C	N
N	F	U	P	R	B	E	I	C	A	L

Name _____

Gingerbread Blends

Complete each word using **sl**, **sn**, or **st**.

___ ice

___ ooze

___ owshoe

___ ocking

___ iffle

___ eeple

___ ar

___ ush

___ eigh

___ uggle

___ ory

___ ed

What does the gingerbread boy have on his bed?

Unscramble these letters to answer the riddle: K O C I O E   S T E S E H

Write your answer on the lines: ___ ___ ___ ___ ___ ___ ___ ___ !

Answer Key

Complete each word using **sl**, **sn**, or **st**.

s **l** ice   **s** **n** ooze   **s** **n** owshoe   **s** **t** ocking   **s** **n** iffle   **s** **t** eeple

s **t** ar   **s** **l** ush   **s** **l** eigh   **s** **n** uggle   **s** **t** ory   **s** **l** ed

What does the gingerbread boy have on his bed?

Unscramble these letters to answer the riddle: K O C I O E   S T E S E H

Write your answer on the lines: <u>C O O K I E</u>   <u>S H E E T S</u> !

48

Two-Wheelin'

Fill in the blanks with **sk, sp,** or **st.**
Write each word on the correct list.

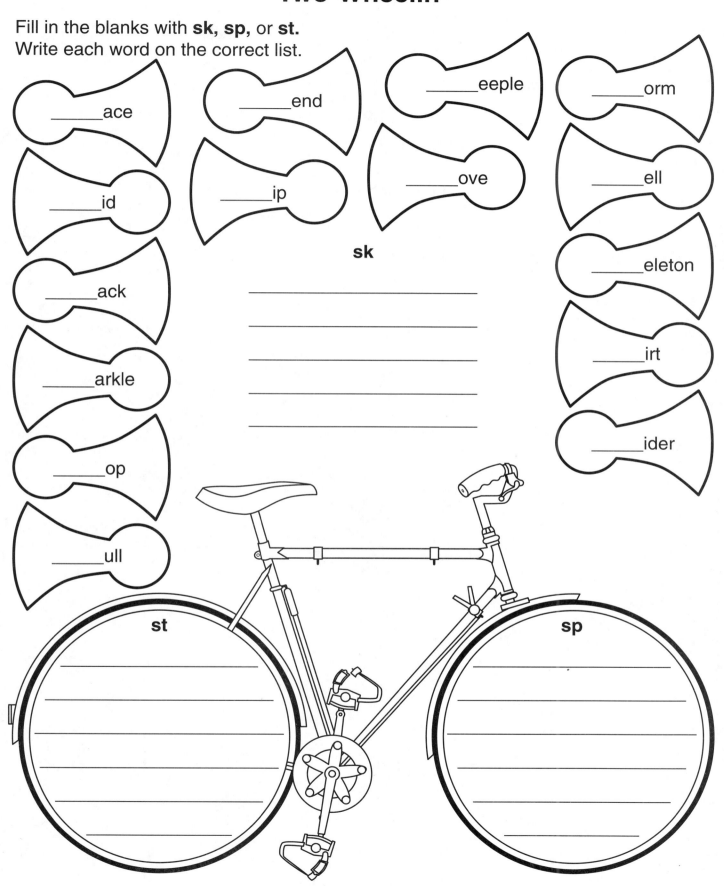

_____ace

_____end

_____eeple

_____orm

_____id

_____ip

_____ove

_____ell

_____ack

sk

_____eleton

_____arkle

_____irt

_____op

_____ider

_____ull

st

sp

Background For The Teacher

May is National Bike Month, established to increase awareness of safe biking rules and proper bicycle maintenance. Some local police departments conduct programs to teach children traffic laws, how to avoid and anticipate hazards, and how to maintain their bikes in good working order.

Extension Activities

— Invite a police officer to speak to the class about bike safety.

— Draw posters illustrating bicycle safety rules. Display in the school halls.
1. Follow all traffic signals.
2. Ride single file on the right side of the street.
3. Have a white light on the front and a danger signal on the rear for night riding.
4. Never hitch a ride on other vehicles.
5. Only have one person on the bicycle at a time.
6. Know and give hand signals.

— Set up a bike inspection station at school where bikers can have their bikes checked for possible hazards. Duplicate awards to be given for good bike maintenance.

Answer Key

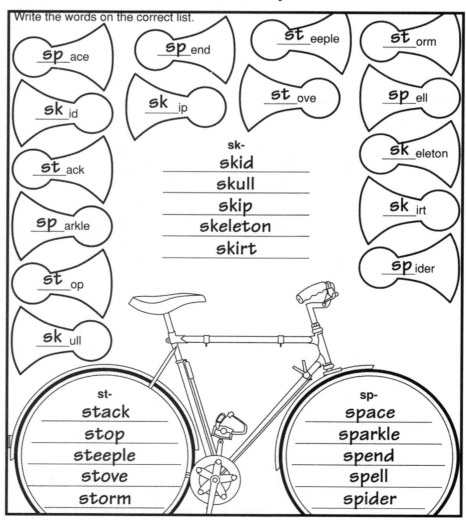

Name _____

Bear's Big Bow

Name the pictures.
Color by the code.

Color Code:
fr —green
cr—yellow
gr—blue
br—red

Sweater Weather

Wiggly Worm is wearing his turtleneck sweater for fall.
Fill in the missing blends and then color Wiggly's sweater.

sm—orange   **sp**—red   **sw**—green
sk—blue   **sn**—yellow **st**—purple

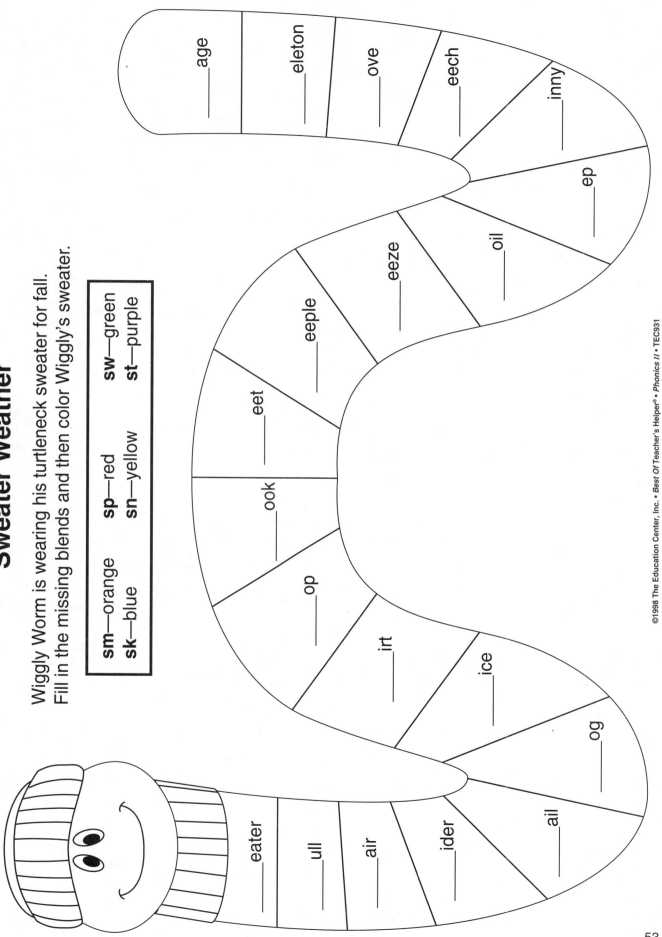

_____ age

_____ eleton

_____ ove

_____ eech

_____ inny

_____ ep

_____ oil

_____ eeze

_____ eeple

_____ eet

_____ ook

_____ op

_____ irt

_____ ice

_____ og

_____ ail

_____ ider

_____ air

_____ ull

_____ eater

Background For The Teacher

On September 22, autumn officially begins in the Northern Hemisphere. The autumnal equinox occurs then, at 3:33 p.m. E.S.T. Except for the areas near the poles, from every place on Earth the sun rises due east and sets due west on that date. Daylight length is also 12 hours and 8 minutes, the same length of time everywhere.

Interestingly, this is the same day that the Southern Hemisphere celebrates its vernal equinox, the beginning of spring.

Extension Activities

— Have students collect fallen autumn leaves to:
  trace around on fall colors of paper.
  press between sheets of waxed paper with a hot iron (with adult supervision).
  place under paper to rub with crayons for montages.
  hold over paper and spatter with tempera paint to create spatter pictures.
  examine, enjoy, and appreciate.

— Brainstorm as a class list of typical autumn activities: hayrides, raking leaves, pulling/tilling/mulching gardens, harvesting crops, drinking hot chocolate, and football games. Create a display with magazine, newspaper, and student-drawn pictures of these activities.

Answer Key

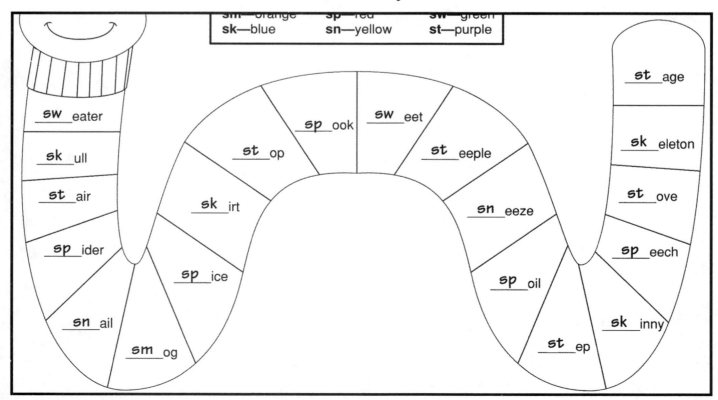

Add-A-Stamp

Color. Cut.
Paste the stamps under the matching beginning blends.

sn

dr

fl

bl

cr

cr

fl

sn

bl

dr

Background For The Teacher

Stamps are printed from engraved steel plates or by a typographic or lithographic process. Some collectors search for rare finds resulting from errors in printing, perforation, adhesive, or paper.

Although the British postal system dates from 1657, the first prepaid, penny adhesive stamp was not used until 1839. Stamp collecting began with this first British issue. In the United States, the first official postage stamp was issued in 1847. Mail delivery in the United States has included the Pony Express from 1860–61, railroad service from 1862, and airmail from 1918. Penny post cards were issued in 1873, and special delivery began in 1885. In 1970 the U.S. Post Office Department was reorganized into the U.S. Postal Service under a postmaster general.

The history of nations can be traced through stamps. The United States prints commemorative stamps to celebrate events or people, memorial stamps, airmail, special delivery, and revenue stamps in addition to regular issues. As a source of revenue, stamps especially attractive to collectors are issued by some countries.

Extension Activities

— Invite a philatelist to show his stamp collection to the class.

— December 3 is the birthday of Sir Rowland Hill, who introduced the adhesive postage stamp in 1839 in Great Britain. Have students design new postage stamps of their own.

— Have interested students collect examples of current postage stamps.

Answer Key

(Since there are two of each blend given, pictures may be under either location for the blend.)

Name _____

I'm Nuts About You!

Fill in the blanks, then color the peanuts.
Use five words to write a story on your own paper.

dri_____

frie_____

au_____

e_____

hau_____

ju_____

po_____

pai_____

sku_____

behi_____

sou_____

blo_____

pri_____

pra_____

ce_____

Answer Key

-nk = brown

dri **nk** brown

frie **nd** orange

au **nt** yellow

e **nd** orange

hau **nt** yellow

ju **nk** brown

po **nd** orange

pai **nt** yellow

sku **nk** brown

behi **nd** orange

sou **nd** orange

blo **nd** orange

pri **nt** yellow

ce **nt** yellow

pra **nk** orange

Name _____

Dreidel Days

Fill in the missing blends.
Then use the words in the sentences below.

spl

scr

str

_____ ash   _____ ub   _____ awberry

_____ atter   _____ eam   _____ eet

_____ it   _____ ape   _____ ipe

_____ ong

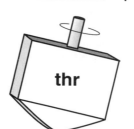

squ

thr

spr

_____ eeze   _____ ow   _____ ead

_____ are   _____ oat   _____ inkle

_____ irrel   _____ ead

1. If you _____ the _____, it will make a mess.

2. It is hard to talk if your _____ hurts.

3. The button stayed in place because the _____ was _____.

4. The _____ ran across the busy _____.

5. I will _____ if you _____ me with water!

6. Please do not _____ the ball in the house.

Background For The Teacher
Hanukkah

Hanukkah, the Festival of Lights, is a Jewish holiday celebrated in December. It begins on the 25th day of the Hebrew month of Kislev and lasts for eight days. This happy holiday celebrates the miraculous victory of a small, untrained Jewish army over the powerful Syrians. About 2,100 years ago, the Syrian king wanted all the people to follow the Greek religion. An elderly priest named Mattathias and his five sons inspired the Jewish people to remain loyal and form a small army to fight the Syrians. The Jewish rebels, called Maccabees, won back the city of Jerusalem and their temple. When the Jews held festivities to rededicate the temple of Jerusalem, they found only enough oil to light their menorah for one day. Miraculously the holy lamp burned for eight days until more oil could be prepared.

To emphasize the joy of the holiday, Jewish children are given gifts each of the eight nights of Hanukkah. They also play with a *dreidel*, a four-sided top. The dreidel is decorated with the Hebrew letters *Nun, Shin, Heh*, and *Gimmel* which say, "A Great Miracle Happened There." Children spin the dreidel to receive tokens, nuts, or wrapped candies.

Extension Activities

— It is a custom for Jews to play games of chance during Hanukkah. Try this Hanukkah word game with your class. Write DREIDEL, HANUKKAH, LATKES, MACCABEE, and MENORAH on a piece of paper. Cut the letters apart and place them in a container. Each student needs a piece of paper with 36 squares on it. (Graph paper may be used.) Call out the letters one at a time. Students record each letter in a square on their paper. After all the letters have been called, students circle the words they have made. The player who has made the most words wins the game.

—Try some tasty Hanukkah potato latkes with this easy recipe.

Grate…	Add…
4 large potatoes	salt and pepper
1 small onion	1 Tbsp. pancake or all-purpose flour
	1 egg
	pinch of baking powder (optional)

Mix together, and fry portions in a skillet over medium heat until they're golden brown.

— The holiday of Hanukkah is a celebration of miracles. Following a discussion about the meaning of the word *miracle,* let children create stories in which a miracle comes true for them.

— Prepare for the Festival of Lights by displaying sparkling stars of David. Provide a pattern for children to trace on white construction paper and cut out. Students paint their stars yellow, then sprinkle them with glitter before the paint dries. When the paint has dried, repeat this procedure on the reverse side. Hang the stars from the ceiling for a shimmering display.

Answer Key

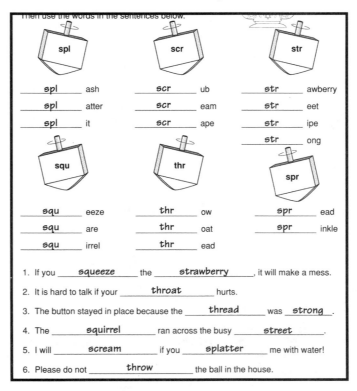

Then use the words in the sentences below.

spl	scr	str
__spl__ ash	__scr__ ub	__str__ awberry
__spl__ atter	__scr__ eam	__str__ eet
__spl__ it	__scr__ ape	__str__ ipe
		__str__ ong

squ	thr	spr
__squ__ eeze	__thr__ ow	__spr__ ead
__squ__ are	__thr__ oat	__spr__ inkle
__squ__ irrel	__thr__ ead	

1. If you __squeeze__ the __strawberry__, it will make a mess.

2. It is hard to talk if your __throat__ hurts.

3. The button stayed in place because the __thread__ was __strong__.

4. The __squirrel__ ran across the busy __street__.

5. I will __scream__ if you __splatter__ me with water!

6. Please do not __throw__ the ball in the house.

Name _____

Gram Quacker's Kitchen

Complete each word using **wr** or **kn**.
Then use the words to fill in the blanks in the sentences.

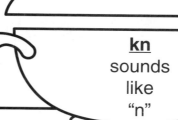

___ ist   ___ uckle   ___ ob   ___ en

___ ock   ___ ench   ___ ee   ___ eck

___ ife   ___ inkle   ___ ight   ___ ot

___ it   ___ ite   ___ ote   ___ ow

___ ong   ___ estle   ___ apsack   ___ eath

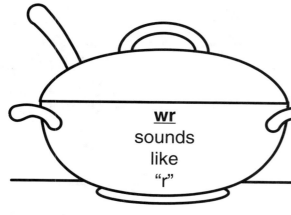

wr sounds like "r"

kn sounds like "n"

1. Did someone _____ on the door?

2. I _____ a letter to my pen pal yesterday.

3. The _____ on my finger hurts.

4. The opposite of right is _____.

5. Be careful with that sharp _____.

6. The little bird singing in the tree is called a _____.

7. Please iron the _____ out of my shirt.

8. I tied a _____ in the rope.

9. My mother used green yarn to _____ my sweater.

10. I did not _____ the answer to the question.

Follow-Up Activity

Have students cross out the words they have used in the sentences at the bottom of the sheet, then write sentences of their own with the remaining words.

Answer Key

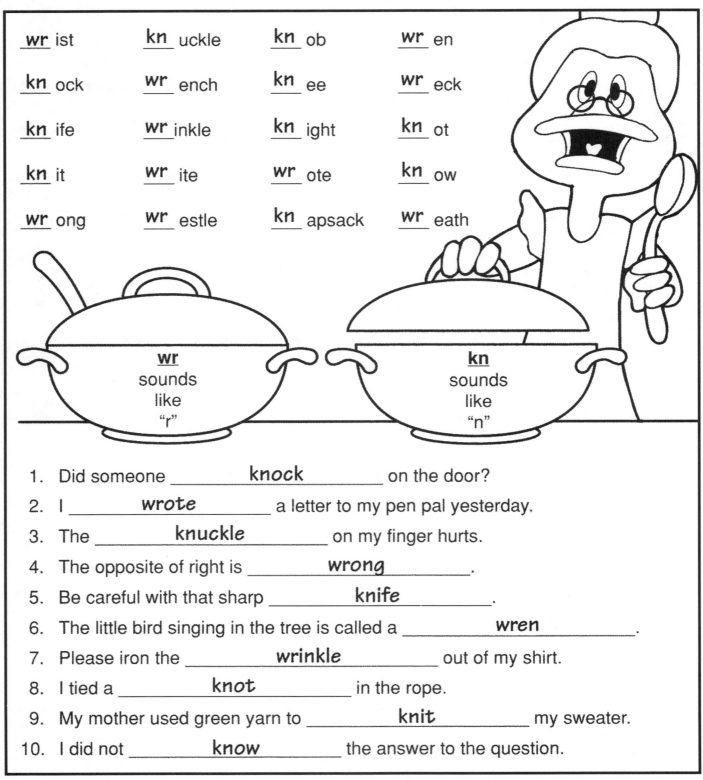

__wr__ ist   __kn__ uckle   __kn__ ob   __wr__ en

__kn__ ock   __wr__ ench   __kn__ ee   __wr__ eck

__kn__ ife   __wr__ inkle   __kn__ ight   __kn__ ot

__kn__ it   __wr__ ite   __wr__ ote   __kn__ ow

__wr__ ong   __wr__ estle   __kn__ apsack   __wr__ eath

wr sounds like "r"

kn sounds like "n"

1. Did someone _____ knock _____ on the door?

2. I _____ wrote _____ a letter to my pen pal yesterday.

3. The _____ knuckle _____ on my finger hurts.

4. The opposite of right is _____ wrong _____.

5. Be careful with that sharp _____ knife _____.

6. The little bird singing in the tree is called a _____ wren _____.

7. Please iron the _____ wrinkle _____ out of my shirt.

8. I tied a _____ knot _____ in the rope.

9. My mother used green yarn to _____ knit _____ my sweater.

10. I did not _____ know _____ the answer to the question.

Name _____

The Great Soup Race

Read each sentence.
Write **wh** or **qu** on the line to complete the missing word.
Fill in the matching circle.

	Scoreboard	
	Quackers	Soupettes
1.	(wh)	(qu)
2.	(wh)	(qu)
3.	(wh)	(qu)
4.	(wh)	(qu)
5.	(wh)	(qu)
6.	(wh)	(qu)
7.	(wh)	(qu)
8.	(wh)	(qu)
9.	(wh)	(qu)
10.	(wh)	(qu)
11.	(wh)	(qu)
12.	(wh)	(qu)
13.	(wh)	(qu)
14.	(wh)	(qu)
15.	(wh)	(qu)

1. Can you answer the ____estion?

2. A ____ale lives in the ocean.

3. Wrap the ____ilt around the baby.

4. We need a ____art of milk from the store.

5. My shoes have black and ____ite stripes.

6. Most kings and ____eens live in castles.

7. When will the farmer harvest his crop of ____eat?

8   This wagon only has three ____eels.

9. I wonder ____at is in the purple box.

10. Did you find that ____arter under your bed?

11. Will we have a ____iz in math today?

12. Sometimes a policeman blows a ____istle.

13. I woke up ____en the doorbell rang.

14. It was very ____iet in the library.

15. That cat has very long ____iskers.

Check the scoreboard to find out which team won the Great Soup Race!
Each • earns one point. Write the name of the winning team on the line.

_____

Fill in the matching circle.

1. Can you answer the _qu_estion?

2. A _wh_ale lives in the ocean.

3. Wrap the _qu_ilt around the baby.

4. We need a _qu_art of milk from the store.

5. My shoes have black and _wh_ite stripes.

6. Most kings and _qu_eens live in castles.

7. When will the farmer harvest his crop of _wh_eat?

8 This wagon only has three _wh_eels.

9. I wonder _wh_at is in the purple box.

10. Did you find that _qu_arter under your bed?

11. Will we have a _qu_iz in math today?

12. Sometimes a policeman blows a _wh_istle.

13. I woke up _wh_en the doorbell rang.

14. It was very _qu_iet in the library.

15. That cat has very long _wh_iskers.

	Quackers	Soupettes
1.	(wh)	(qu)
2.	(wh)	(qu)
3.	(wh)	(qu)
4.	(wh)	(qu)
5.	(wh)	(qu)
6.	(wh)	(qu)
7.	(wh)	(qu)
8.	(wh)	(qu)
9.	(wh)	(qu)
10.	(wh)	(qu)
11.	(wh)	(qu)
12.	(wh)	(qu)
13.	(wh)	(qu)
14.	(wh)	(qu)
15.	(wh)	(qu)

Check the scoreboard to find out which team won the Great Soup Race!
Each • earns one point. Write the name of the winning team on the line.
Quackers

Name _____

Bat Collections

Bonnie and Barney collect words.
Help Bonnie and Barney by completing each word with **ch**, **sh**, or **th**.
Then write each word in the correct jar.

fi _____   tea _____   pa _____   pea _____

sou _____   wa _____   bru _____   lun _____

mon _____   spla _____   tee _____   whi _____

ch

sh

th

Bonus Box: On the back of this sheet, write a sentence telling about what you would like to collect. Draw a picture to go with the sentence.

Answer Key

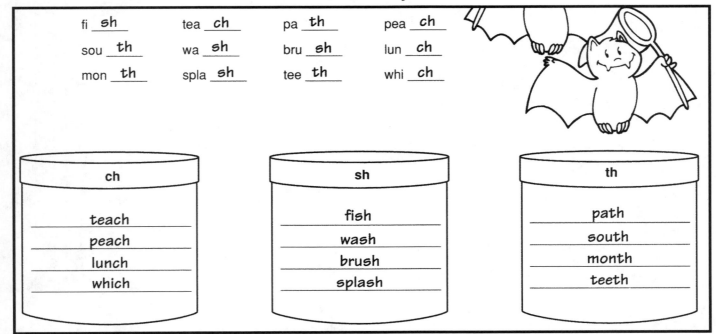

fi **sh**   tea **ch**   pa **th**   pea **ch**

sou **th**   wa **sh**   bru **sh**   lun **ch**

mon **th**   spla **sh**   tee **th**   whi **ch**

ch
teach
peach
lunch
which

sh
fish
wash
brush
splash

th
path
south
month
teeth

Consonant digraphs: *ch, sh, th, wh*

Mother's Little Helpers

Fill in the missing digraphs. Then write the words on the aprons.

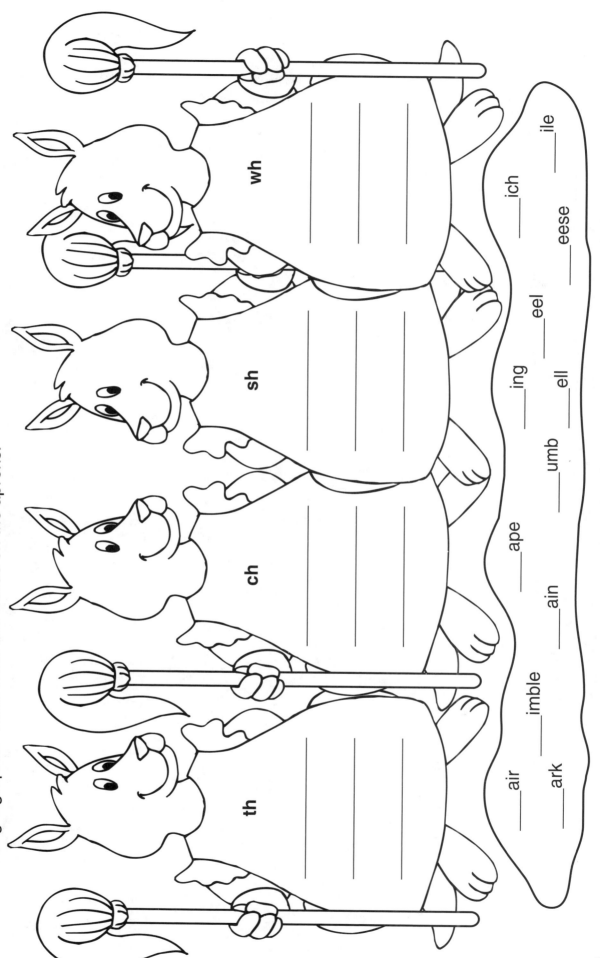

wh   sh   ch   th

air   imble   ape   ain   umb   ing   ell   eel   ich   ile

ark   ain   ape   umb   ell   eese

Background For The Teacher

By presidential proclamation, Mother's Day is always the second Sunday in May. It was first observed in 1907 in Philadelphia, when Anna Jarvis suggested that her church hold a memorial service for all mothers.

On Mother's Day we remember our mothers and may show our appreciation by giving gifts of flowers, candy, or special Mother's Day greetings. Some people take Mom out to dinner or help out with household chores.

Extension Activities

— Have children cut out magazine pictures of animal mothers and their babies. Paste on folded paper to create humorous Mother's Day cards.

— Design awards for children to give to their Super Moms.

— Have students bring in snapshots of themselves as babies. Take snapshots of individual students, and place both photos side by side in a plastic pocket. Mount each pocket on construction paper and decorate with lace, ribbon, or dried, pressed flowers for a Mother's Day gift.

— Choose an easy candy recipe for children to make in class to take home to their mothers.

Answer Key

Name _____

An Apple A Day

Finish each word on the basket.
Write the digraph **ch, sh, th,** or **wh** on the lines.
Then copy each word onto the matching apple.

ch   **sh**   **th**   **wh**

___ est   ___ eel   ___ amp   pu ___   ___ ing
___ bru   ___ iver   ___ isper   ___ irty   ___ ell
mat ___   ___ ed   ___ ange   ___ iff   ben ___

69

Answer Key

ch	sh	th · wh
champ	push	thing
chest	shell	wheel
bench	shiver	thirty
change	brush	whisper
match	shed	whiff

t h ing	pu s h	c h amp	w h eel	c h est
s h ell	t h irty	w h isper	s h iver	bru s h
ben c h	w h iff	c h ange	s h ed	mat c h

Consonant digraphs: *ch, sh, th, wh*

Pack A Picnic!

Fill in the blank in each word with the correct digraph: **ch**, **wh**, **sh**, or **th**.
Then list the word on the matching basket.
Beside each word write the food on which the word was found.
You should have one food from each food group in each basket.

____ought — cereal

____ap — pineapple

____eel — yogurt

____are — milk

____umb — cheese

____imney — butter

th
food
word

sh
food
word

____ile — roll

____ape — fish

____eet — banana

____ite — chicken

wh
food
word

ch
food
word

____ill — cracker

____eese — turkey

____ich — apple

____ankful — carrot

____one — bread

____em — steak

©1998 The Education Center, Inc. • *Best Of Teacher's Helper® • Phonics II* • TEC931

Background For The Teacher

National Nutrition Month is recognized from March 1–31 each year. The purpose of this special month is to give the general public the best available information about nutrition and food selection for good physical health.

Excellent teaching materials on nutrition are available from your local branch of the National Dairy Council, as well as many other groups.

Extension Activity

— Interesting topics for classroom discussion on nutrition:

Snacks and snacktimes
Meals at school
Reasons for eating
How advertising influences eating habits
Favorite foods
Holidays, special days, and foods
Food fads
Family get-togethers and foods
Foods from around the world
Health foods and healthful foods
The food pyramid
Nutrients in food
Eyes, skin, hair, teeth, and nutrition
Fast-food menus

Answer Key

	WORD	FOOD		WORD	FOOD
WH	which	apple	TH	thankful	carrot
	white	chicken		them	steak
	wheel	yogurt		thumb	cheese
	while	roll		thought	cereal
CH	chill	cracker	SH	shone	bread
	cheese	turkey		sheet	banana
	chap	pineapple		share	milk
	chimney	butter		shape	fish

Name _____

Piñata Party

Fill in the blanks with **ch, sh, th,** or **wh.**

CRACK!

_____oe

_____air

_____urch

_____isper

_____ark

_____ree

_____irt

_____eel

_____ain

_____ite

_____ing

_____ild

_____ell

_____umb

_____is

Background For The Teacher

In Mexico and parts of the American Southwest, the piñata is part of the Christmas festivities. A large clay or papier-mâché jar, sometimes shaped like an animal or a character, is filled with candies and fruit. Children, in turn, swing at the piñata with a stick to break it open and release a shower of treats.

Answer Key

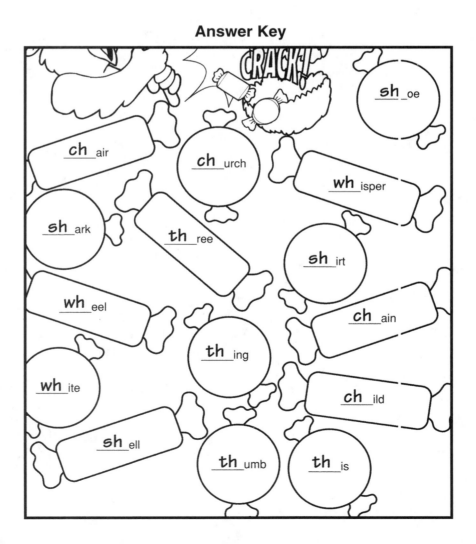

Bumps And Bruises

Look at the words on each rabbit's skis.
Write the matching contraction on each line.
Use the words in the Word Box.

_____   _____   _____

_____   _____   _____

_____   _____   _____

Word Box

let's	don't
isn't	here's
you're	she'll
couldn't	there's
who'd	I'm
they'll	

_____   _____

Bonus Box: Circle the letters in
the words on the skis above that
are *replaced* by the apostrophe.

Answer Key

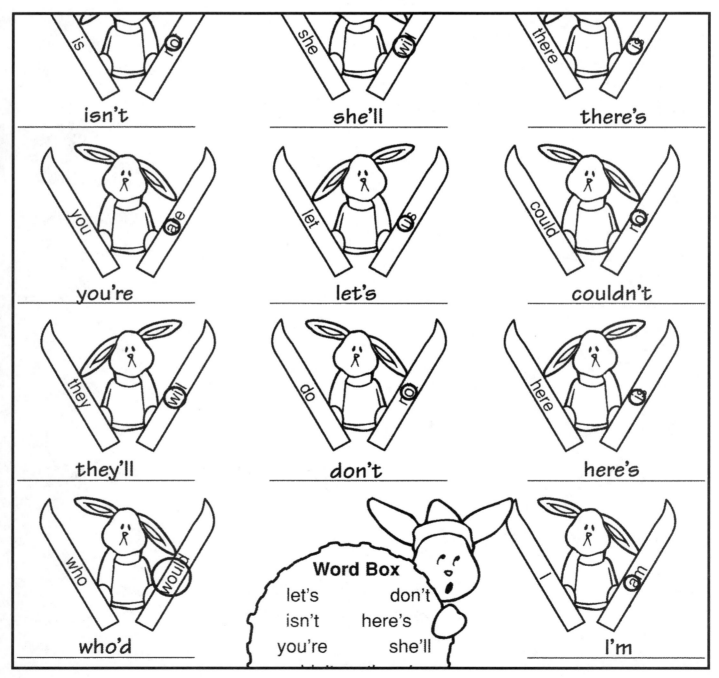

isn't

she'll

there's

you're

let's

couldn't

they'll

don't

here's

who'd

Word Box

let's   don't

isn't   here's

you're   she'll

I'm

Abe's Collection Of Contractions

Write the contraction for each word pair on the line.
Circle the letter or letters in each word pair that you left out.

Remember that when two words are written together as a contraction, you see an apostrophe to show where some letters have been left out.

1. are n(o)t   _aren't_____

2. he would   _____

3. we are   _____

4. you have   _____

5. she will   _____

6. would not   _____

7. they have   _____

8. they would   _____

9. you are   _____

10. it will   _____

11. had not   _____

12. let us   _____

13. I am   _____

14. you will   _____

15. I would   _____

16. does not   _____

Bonus Box: Abraham Lincoln loved to read. By reading he learned many things. On the back of this sheet, write down the title of your favorite book. Then write one sentence that tells what this book is about.

Follow-Up Activities

— Have students write the list of contractions in ABC order.
— Have students use each contraction in a sentence of its own.

Background For The Teacher

Abraham Lincoln was born in a dirt-floor log cabin in Hodgenville, Kentucky on February 12, 1809. He lived in Kentucky, Indiana, and Illinois. With probably less than one year of formal education, he taught himself to read and closely studied the family Bible. As a boy, he split log fence rails, plowed fields, cut corn, and threshed wheat. He often entertained others with his speaking talent. Later, he clerked in a store, served in the military, and earned his license to practice law.

His presidency spanned March 4, 1861–April 14, 1865, the Civil War era. On April 14, five days after General Lee's surrender, he was shot by John Wilkes Booth and died the next day.

Answer Key

1.	are not	aren't
2.	he would	he'd
3.	we are	we're
4.	you have	you've
5.	she will	she'll
6.	would not	wouldn't
7.	they have	they've
8.	they would	they'd
9.	you are	you're
10.	it will	it'll
11.	had not	hadn't
12.	let us	let's
13.	I am	I'm
14.	you will	you'll
15.	I would	I'd
16.	does not	doesn't

Name _____

Snow Bunny Fun ❄

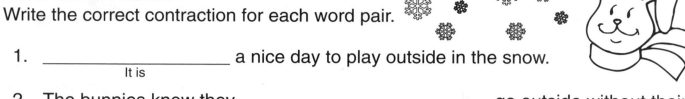

Read each sentence.
Write the correct contraction for each word pair.

1. _____ a nice day to play outside in the snow.
   It is

2. The bunnies know they _____ go outside without their
   should not
   hats and mittens.

3. Fuzzy's friends said _____ bring their sleds over this
   they would
   afternoon.

4. "_____ the best place to go sledding?" asked Hoppy.
   Where is

5. Fluffy _____ want to slide down the big hill.
   does not

6. Floppy said, "_____ slide down the big hill!"
   I will

7. Hoppy said _____ go down the little hill with Fluffy.
   she would

8. Fluffy _____ pull the sled up the slippery hill without
   could not
   falling.

9. It _____ stopped snowing all day.
   has not

10. The bunnies _____ had so much fun in a long time!
    have not

11. "_____ we going to have hot chocolate when we go inside?"
    Are not

12. "_____ have some cookies, too!" added Floppy.
    Let us

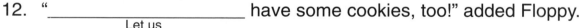

Bonus Box: On another sheet of paper, write a story about the perfect winter day. Use one or more contractions in your story. Draw a picture for your story.

Answer Key

1. <u>It's</u> a nice day to play outside in the snow.
2. The bunnies know they <u>shouldn't</u> go outside without their hats and mittens.
3. Fuzzy's friends said <u>they'd</u> bring their sleds over this afternoon.
4. "<u>Where's</u> the best place to go sledding?" asked Hoppy.
5. Fluffy <u>doesn't</u> want to slide down the big hill.
6. Floppy said, "<u>I'll</u> slide down the big hill!"
7. Hoppy said <u>she'd</u> go down the little hill with Fluffy.
8. Fluffy <u>couldn't</u> pull the sled up the slippery hill without falling.
9. It <u>hasn't</u> stopped snowing all day.
10. The bunnies <u>haven't</u> had so much fun in a long time!
11. Fuzzy asked, "<u>Aren't</u> we going to have hot chocolate when we go inside?"
12. "<u>Let's</u> have some cookies, too!" added Floppy.

Name _____

Party Time!

Read each sentence.
Write the correct contraction for each word pair.

1. _____ Todd and Tina's birthday.
   It is

2. "_____ have a tree party!" said Todd.
   Let us

3. "Some of our friends _____ fly," Tina reminded him.
   can not

4. "_____ we have a party by the river?" she asked.
   Could not

5. "_____ a great idea!" said Todd.
   That is

6. "_____ going to tell everyone," he said.
   I am

7. Tina said _____ get everything ready.
   she would

8. _____ have to hurry.
   She will

9. She _____ have much time.
   will not

10. Todd _____ gone long.
    was not

11. All of their friends said _____ come.
    they would

12. When everyone had arrived, Tina said, "_____ lots of cake!"
    There is

13. "_____ like ice cream?" Todd asked.
    Who would

14. "_____ you going to open your presents?" called their friends.
    Are not

15. "_____ never had so much fun!" they said.
    We have

16. Todd and Tina _____ want their party to end.
    did not

Bonus Box: On another sheet of paper, write a story about a party that you have had or would like to have. Use one or more contractions in your story. Draw a picture to go with the story.

How To Use The Award Below

Duplicate copies of the award. When a child successfully completes his toucan worksheet, staple a personalized award to his paper.

Award

As Bright As A Toucan...

Look what you can do!

Good work, _____!

_____

Name _____

Pile Of Presents!

Use the words on each gift to make a contraction.
Write each contraction on the correct line below.

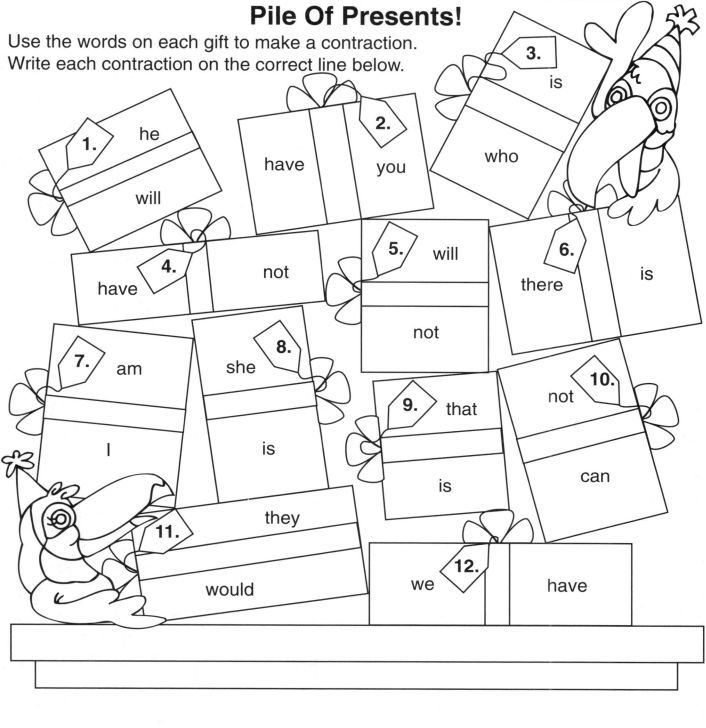

1. _____ 5. _____ 9. _____

2. _____ 6. _____ 10. _____

3. _____ 7. _____ 11. _____

4. _____ 8. _____ 12. _____

Bonus Box: On the back of this sheet, draw a picture of a gift you would like to receive. Write a sentence about it. Use a contraction in your sentence.

Answer Key

1. he'll	5. won't	9. that's
2. you've	6. there's	10. can't
3. who's	7. I'm	11. they'd
4. haven't	8. she's	12. we've

Name _____

Snow Bunnies And Friends

Look at the words on the snowmen.
Write three contractions using each word and words in the Word Bank.

I

she

we

you

Word Bank

am   have   is   will   are   would

Bonus Box: Draw a picture of yourself making a snowman. Write a sentence about your picture. Use a contraction in your sentence.

Answer Key

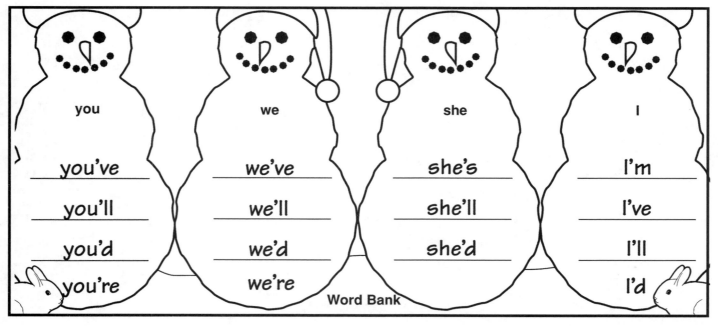

you	we	she	I
you've	we've	she's	I'm
you'll	we'll	she'll	I've
you'd	we'd	she'd	I'll
you're	we're		I'd

Word Bank

Name _____

It's All In The Way You Slice It

Find the compound word in each row.
Draw a line between the two words in each compound word.
Write the words on the lines below.
The first one is done for you.

1. yesterday   window   doll|house
2. tablecloth   brother   together
3. ladder   backyard   bigger
4. goldfish   running   bottle
5. standing   bicycle   homework
6. picture   cowgirl   washer
7. butterfly   circus   little
8. spelling   hurry   dishpan
9. father   hairbrush   bigger
10. bathroom   funny   kitchen
11. reading   playground   table
12. highway   science   story

1. _doll_ _____   _house_ _____
2. _____   _____
3. _____   _____
4. _____   _____
5. _____   _____
6. _____   _____
7. _____   _____
8. _____   _____
9. _____   _____
10. _____   _____
11. _____   _____
12. _____   _____

Extension Activities
Compound Words

— Make a compound word game by writing the individual component words of compound words on index cards. (See page 92 for a list of compound words.) Deal five cards to each player, leaving the remainder of the cards in the deck. Players take turns selecting cards from the deck, then laying down card pairs that form compound words. The first player to lay down all of his cards wins.

— Use the same index cards (see above) to play another compound word game. Give each student a card. Instruct students to pair up with other students to form compound words. Student pairs should then sit down and compose sentences using their compound words. When all students are seated, have student pairs share their compound words and sentences with the rest of the class.

Answer Key

1.	yesterday	window	dollhouse
2.	tablecloth	brother	together
3.	ladder	backyard	bigger
4.	goldfish	running	bottle
5.	standing	bicycle	homework
6.	picture	cowgirl	washer
7.	butterfly	circus	little
8.	spelling	hurry	dishpan
9.	father	hairbrush	bigger
10.	bathroom	funny	kitchen
11.	reading	playground	table
12.	highway	science	story

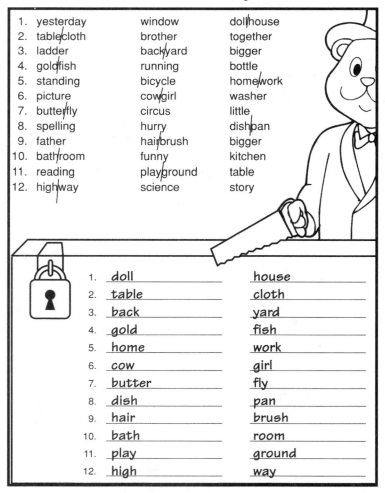

1.	doll	house
2.	table	cloth
3.	back	yard
4.	gold	fish
5.	home	work
6.	cow	girl
7.	butter	fly
8.	dish	pan
9.	hair	brush
10.	bath	room
11.	play	ground
12.	high	way

Name _____

Abracadabra!

Can you pull a compound word out of a hat?
Read the words in each hat.
Use two of the words to make a compound word.
Write the compound word on the line.

1. _____

sun
leg
flower

2. _____

rail
barn
road

3. _____

brush
tooth
car

4. _____

side
rain
walk

5. _____

up
stairs
desk

6. _____

tree
two
house

7. _____

yellow
corn
pop

8. _____

way
base
ball

9. _____

boat
cake
pan

10. _____

works
up
fire

11. _____

box
mail
moon

12. _____

run
ship
space

Bonus Box: Write a story called "The Best Magic Trick Ever". Use at least three of the compound words from above in your story.

Answer Key

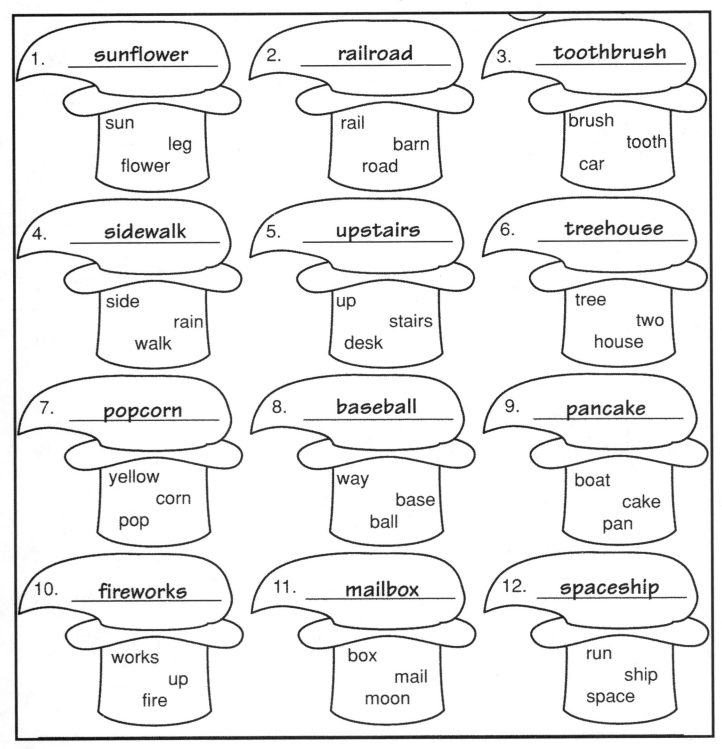

1. __sunflower__

   sun

   leg

   flower

2. __railroad__

   rail

   barn

   road

3. __toothbrush__

   brush

   tooth

   car

4. __sidewalk__

   side

   rain

   walk

5. __upstairs__

   up

   stairs

   desk

6. __treehouse__

   tree

   two

   house

7. __popcorn__

   yellow

   corn

   pop

8. __baseball__

   way

   base

   ball

9. __pancake__

   boat

   cake

   pan

10. __fireworks__

   works

   up

   fire

11. __mailbox__

   box

   mail

   moon

12. __spaceship__

   run

   ship

   space

Name _____

Compound words

Compound Word Juggle

How well can you juggle?
Read the words in the balls.
Two of the words can be used in each
sentence to make two compound words.
Cross out the word that cannot be used.
Write one word on the line to finish each
sentence.

For example:

I had to push my bike __up__ hill.
or, I had to push my bike _down_ hill.

1. I put the _____ boat in the water.

2. I left my book in the _____ room.

3. I love to eat _____ bread.

4. Let's play _____ ball.

5. I left my comb in the _____ room.

6. May I write on the _____ board?

©1998 The Education Center, Inc. • *Best Of* Teacher's Helper® • *Phonics II* • TEC931

Compound Word List

Use with the extension activities listed on page 88.

afternoon	everybody	playground	butterfly	homemade	somebody
airplane	fingerprint	popcorn	campfire	homework	someday
anyone	firewood	quarterback	cannot	horseback	spaceship
anything	fireworks	rattlesnake	cheeseburger	horseshoe	starfish
backbone	football	raincoat	classmate	houseboat	suitcase
backyard	footprint	railroad	classroom	lighthouse	sunrise
baseball	goldfish	rowboat	doorbell	mailbox	sunset
basketball	grandfather	schoolhouse	doorway	moonlight	sunshine
bathroom	hairbrush	seashell	downhill	newspaper	textbook
bathtub	handshake	seashore	downstairs	notebook	underline
bedroom	handwriting	snowball	downtown	paintbrush	waterfall
blackboard	highway	snowflake	eggshell	pancake	weekend

Answer Key

1. I put the <u>sail/row</u> boat in the water.

2. I left my book in the <u>bed/class</u> room.

3. I love to eat <u>ginger/corn</u> bread.

4. Let's play <u>foot/base</u> ball.

5. I left my comb in the <u>bath/bed</u> room.

6. May I write on the <u>black/chalk</u> board?

Name _____

Christmas Compounds

Make compound words.
Write the compound words
on the poinsettias.

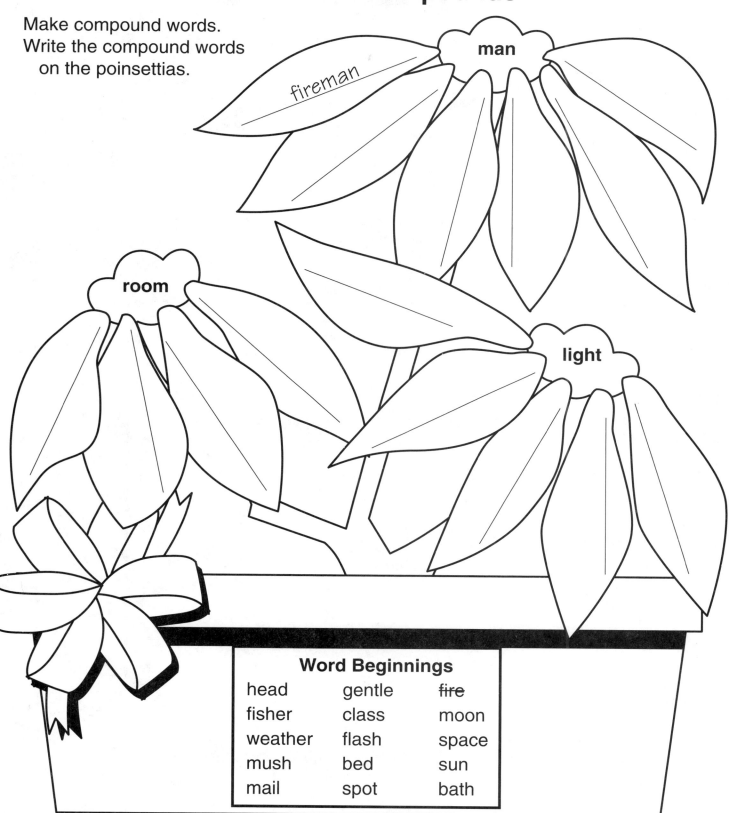

fireman

man

room

light

Word Beginnings

head	gentle	~~fire~~
fisher	class	moon
weather	flash	space
mush	bed	sun
mail	spot	bath

Bonus Box: Color the insides of the flowers yellow. Trace around the petals with your red crayon.
On the back of this sheet, write why you think the poinsettia is a Christmas flower.

Variations

— White-out the word beginnings, word endings, and directions. Program the poinsettia middles with the plural endings *s, es,* and *ies.* Program the poinsettia pot with appropriate singular words.

— White-out the word beginnings, word endings, lines, and directions. Then program using one of the following examples.
  • Fill poinsettia centers with math answers and the poinsettia pot with corresponding math problems.
  • Fill poinsettia centers with missing addends, subtrahends, or factors. Fill the poinsettia pot with corresponding math problems.
  • Fill all poinsettia parts with math problems. Program the poinsettia pot with a color code.

Answer Key

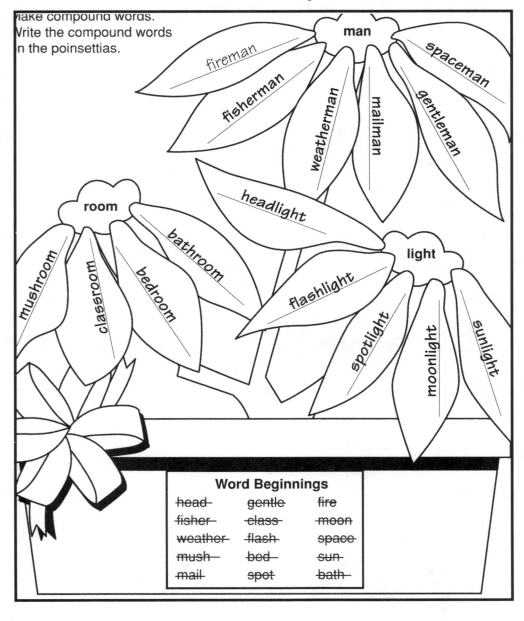

Make compound words. Write the compound words in the poinsettias.

man — fireman, fisherman, weatherman, mailman, gentleman, spaceman

room — mushroom, classroom, bedroom, bathroom

light — headlight, flashlight, spotlight, moonlight, sunlight

Word Beginnings

head	gentle	fire
fisher	class	moon
weather	flash	space
mush	bed	sun
mail	spot	bath

Name _____

Compound Critters

A mother opossum carries her babies on her back.
Cut and glue the babies to the matching mothers to make compound words.

hill

how

stairs

set

shine

body

town

where

rise

down

sun

some

Answer Key

sunrise	downhill	somewhere
sunset	downstairs	somehow
sunshine	downtown	somebody

Name _____

For "Eggs-perts" Only!

Add the same word to all of the words in each egg.
On the lines write the four compound words that you make.

1.
mat
man
knob
bell

_____
_____
_____
_____

2.
fire
house
butter
horse

_____
_____
_____
_____

3.
suit
pillow
show
book

_____
_____
_____
_____

4.
star
gold
sword
cat

_____
_____
_____
_____

5.
ball
storm
drift
fall

_____
_____
_____
_____

6.
black
checker
game
wash

_____
_____
_____
_____

7.
pen
time
ground
mate

_____
_____
_____
_____

8.
ship
lumber
barn
stock

_____
_____
_____
_____

Bonus Box: Use your markers or crayons to decorate this egg. Make it look like no other decorated egg you've ever seen!

Answer Key

1.	2.	3.
doormat	firefly	suitcase
doorman	housefly	pillowcase
doorknob	butterfly	showcase
doorbell	horsefly	bookcase

4.	5.	6.
starfish	snowball	blackboard
goldfish	snowstorm	checkerboard
swordfish	snowdrift	gameboard
catfish	snowfall	washboard

7.	8.
playpen	shipyard
playtime	lumberyard
playground	barnyard
playmate	stockyard

Name _____

Bunny Trail

Easter Bunny hid the eggs so well that he can't find his way home! Help him out by drawing eggs ⬭ around the **compound words.** Then trace the path to his house!

START

looking

eggshell

flowerpot

hidden

downhill

daybreak

grasshopper

dozen

singing

basket

clump

paintbrush

carried

colored

hillside

hurry

backyard

finding

grassy

birdbath

sunshine

E. Bunny

Background For The Teacher

In the Northern Hemisphere, Easter comes on or after the full moon of the spring equinox. Thus the Easter season is also associated with spring, the season of nature's rebirth.

Some Easter customs evolved from pre-Christian beliefs. In ancient times the egg symbolized the miracle of new life. Chinese people still give painted, red eggs to friends to announce the birth of a son or daughter. Some people believed that Easter eggs had magical powers. Dyeing and decorating eggs with good-luck symbols and special designs became an art in eastern Europe. The eggs were blessed at church and given to friends and relatives.

Baby chicks and lambs also represent new life and hope. Lambs were sacrificed in the ancient Jewish Passover ceremony. In the Christian religion, the lamb became a symbol of Jesus, who sacrificed his life.

The Easter bunny who delivers decorated eggs combines the rabbit, symbol of fertility, with the good luck of Easter eggs. In German-speaking countries, children build special nests or gardens for the Easter "hare." In South America, a painted rabbit brings Easter eggs.

Extension Activities

— Create egg people for an Easter-egg tree. Hang plastic eggs, decorated with wiggle eyes and yarn hair, from a tree branch anchored in a flowerpot.

— Design Easter bonnets using white paper plates, crepe paper, lace, ribbon, fabric scraps, and artificial flowers.

— Make a display of different kinds of Easter eggs—candy, dyed, wooden, glass, sugar, plastic.

— Have students examine and plant bulbs or force a cutting from a flowering shrub by bringing it inside so it will bloom early.

— Ask the owner of a pet rabbit to share it with the class for one day. Discuss its care and food requirements. Display pictures of different kinds of rabbits in the wild.

— Obtain and incubate a chicken egg. Make a calendar to record temperature and developments during the 21 days required. Discuss how baby chicks hatch and precautions needed. Plan ahead to place the hatched chick in a suitable home.

Answer Key

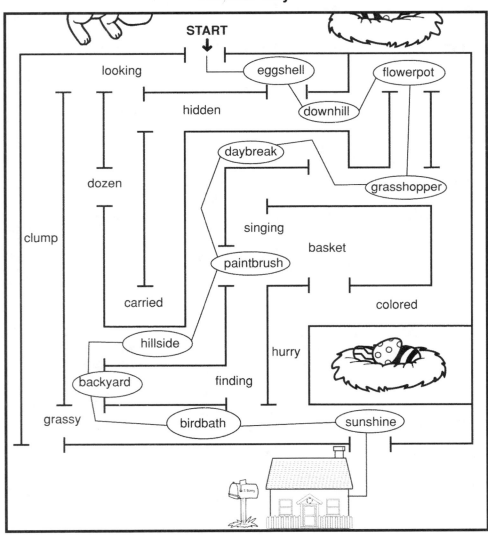

Name _____

Campfire Compounds

Color only the compound word tents.

compass

troop

cookout

wildlife

scoutmaster

badge

hiking

backpack

dinner

campground

patrol

pathfinder

teamwork

swimming

tenderfoot

lifeguard

scouting

firewood

Background For The Teacher

The Boy Scouts of America were created in 1908 in Great Britain by Sir Robert Baden-Powell and were incorporated in the United States in 1910. Boy Scouting has organizations all over the world. Scouts meet at international camp-outs called Boy Scout jamborees.

Scouting emphasizes mental, moral, and physical development through outdoor skills, crafts, and citizenship. Community troops are divided into patrols of ten boys each, led by an adult scoutmaster. In 1930 Cub Scouting was started for younger boys ages 7–10.

Answer Key

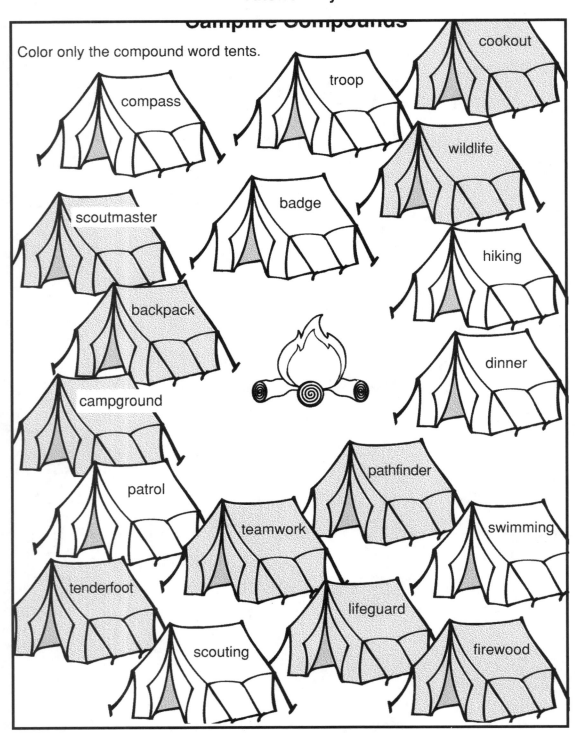

Campfire Compounds

Color only the compound word tents.

compass · troop · cookout · wildlife · badge · scoutmaster · hiking · backpack · dinner · campground · patrol · teamwork · pathfinder · swimming · tenderfoot · lifeguard · firewood · scouting

Name _____

Petey's Icebreakers

Help Petey break the ice blocks in half.
Read each compound word.
Draw a line between the words.
The first one is done for you.

air|plane

outdoor

eyelid

treetop

catfish

mailbox

birdbath

forget

raindrop

icebox

backyard

cowboy

sailboat

Bonus Box: On the back of this sheet, scramble five compound words. Have a friend unscramble them!

Answer Key

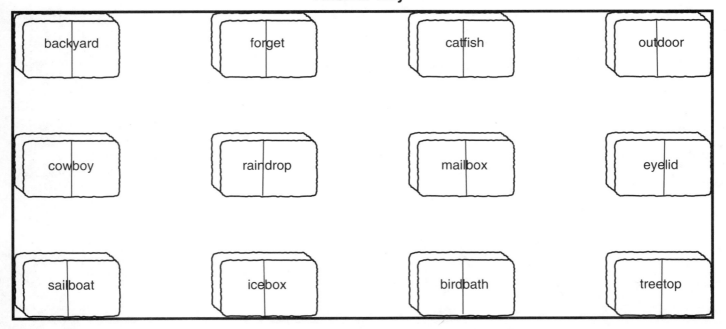

Name _____

Sorting The Mail

Look at the words on each envelope.
If the words are **synonyms**, write the
words on the **"To Be Delivered"** mailbag.
If the words are **not synonyms**, write the
words on the **"Return To Sender"** mailbag.

Remember! Synonyms are words that have about the same meaning.

soggy
wet

little
big

huge
large

work
play

tidy
neat

first
last

loud
noisy

fast
quick

near
far

stop
start

To Be Delivered

_____
_____
_____
_____

Return To Sender

_____
_____
_____
_____

Answer Key

(The order of answers in each column may vary.)

To Be Delivered	Return To Sender
soggy—wet	little—big
huge—large	work—play
tidy—neat	first—last
loud—noisy	near—far
fast—quick	stop—start

Name _____

Handsome Harry

Handsome Harry wants words that aren't overused.
On the hats below, write **synonyms** for the overused words.
On the back of this sheet, use each new word in a sentence.
  (Try to find <u>unusual</u> synonyms.)

1. good

2. said

3. nice

4. wow

5. asked

6. think

7. like

8. bad

9. hate

10. love

Extension Activities

— Plan an Old West day. Students come in costume for a rodeo parade or creative dramatics.

— Invite a Native American to speak to the class.

— Play a Pony Express relay game. Discuss mail delivery by stagecoach, train, or rider.

— Read *Little House On The Prairie* by Laura Ingalls Wilder. Have students create dioramas of their favorite scenes.

— Research and map famous routes to the West such as the Santa Fé and Oregon trails.

— Pack a covered wagon for the journey west. List items you would take on a large cut-out covered wagon. Discuss reasons for being selective.

— Make sourdough bread or pancakes.

— Pan for gold. Demonstrate the technique. Display samples of ores.

— Learn cowboy songs for a "campfire" program.

— List vocabulary for creative writing.

saddle	chaps	gold rush
boots	holster	bronco
spurs	stirrups	longhorn steer
ten-gallon hat	canteen	branding iron
stagecoach	bandana	
ghost town	lariat	

— Have each child create an original brand for his own ranch.

Name _____

Skating Party

Read the word on each skate.
Find each word's synonym in the Word Bank.
Write a synonym on each skate.

cool

beach

talk

icy

happy

fly

pick

pretty

sea

windy

loud

coarse

Word Bank

lovely	rough	choose
speak	chilly	breezy
noisy	ocean	soar
shore	frozen	glad

Remember: **Synonyms** are words that have almost the same meaning.

Bonus Box: Put the words in the Word Bank in ABC order.

©1998 The Education Center, Inc. • *Best Of Teacher's Helper® • Phonics II* • TEC931

109

Extension Activities
Synonyms

— Instead of a spelling bee, why not try a synonym bee? Using spelling words, reading vocabulary words, or content area words, children must give a synonym for each given word. For variety, don't forget to hold an antonym bee!

— Challenge your students to work in small groups to prepare illustrations of words with multiple meanings. For example, if a team has the word *bat,* they would use crayons, colored pencils, or markers to draw the animal *bat* and a baseball *bat.* Use the following list to get you started:

bat	litter	dribble	pen	pop	ring
box	fall	check	tie	cut	shop

— Have your children make vocabulary eggs. Each child will need one stocking egg and ten strips of colored paper. Each child writes five words and their synonyms (or antonyms), one word per strip. Place the word strips inside the egg. Store the eggs in a basket. Children match word strips for fun vocabulary practice.

Answer Key

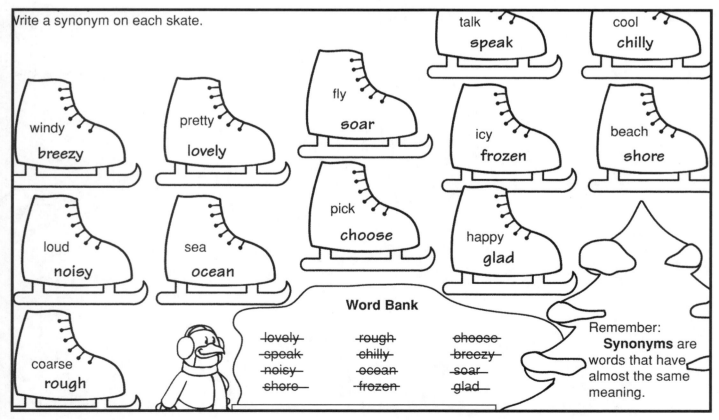

Write a synonym on each skate.

talk — speak
cool — chilly
windy — breezy
pretty — lovely
fly — soar
icy — frozen
beach — shore
loud — noisy
sea — ocean
pick — choose
happy — glad
coarse — rough

Word Bank

lovely · rough · choose
speak · chilly · breezy
noisy · ocean · soar
shore · frozen · glad

Remember: **Synonyms** are words that have almost the same meaning.

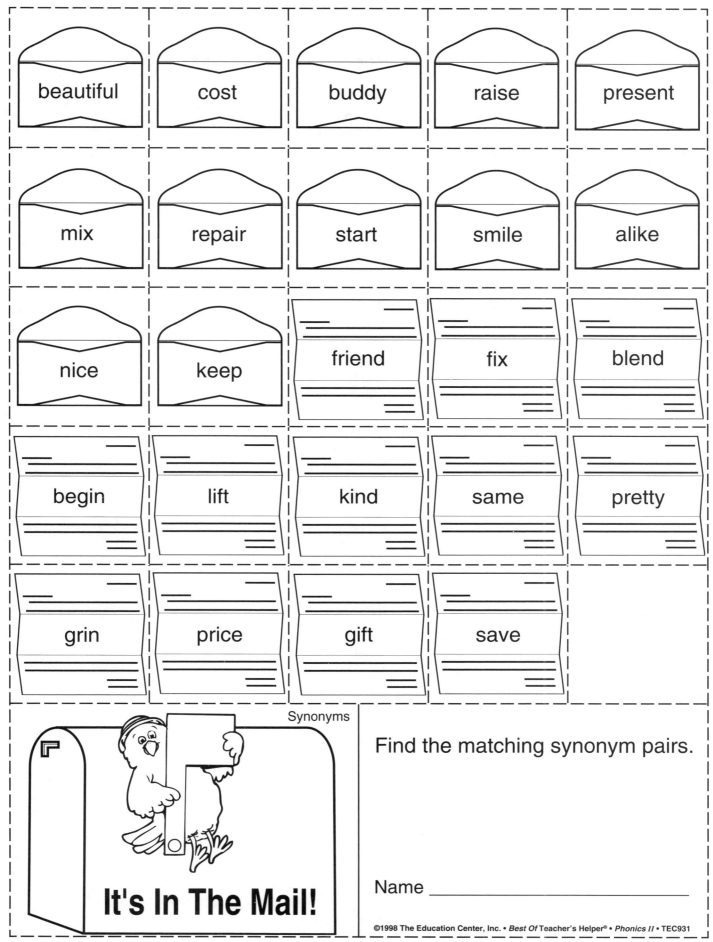

beautiful	cost	buddy	raise	present
mix	repair	start	smile	alike
nice	keep	friend	fix	blend
begin	lift	kind	same	pretty
grin	price	gift	save	

Synonyms

Find the matching synonym pairs.

It's In The Mail!

Name _____

Materials Needed

— scissors
— glue

How To Use Page 111

Provide students with construction-paper copies of page 111. Have students cut out the game pieces and mailbox along the dotted lines. To create mailboxes, have the students fold their mailbox pieces in half along the line. Then have students apply thin layers of glue along the inside top and bottom edges of their mailbox pieces as shown and press the halves together. Set aside to dry. (Allow students to color the mailboxes if desired.) To play, students match the 12 synonym pairs. Store the game pieces inside the mailboxes when not in use. Encourage students to take their games home for further practice.

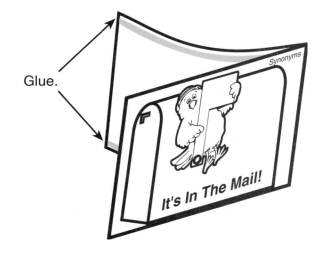

Glue.

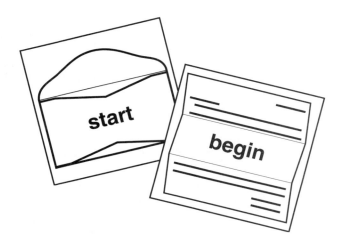

Name _____

Larry's Love Letter

Help Larry write a letter to Lucy.
Look at the Word Bank.
Write the correct synonym in each blank.

Remember:
Synonyms are words
that have the same or
almost the same meanings.

Word Bank

glad	leaps
story	harm
smile	protect
friend	beautiful
beside	nice

Bonus Box: On the back of this sheet, write
two more pairs of synonyms. Then write a
sentence using each word.

Dear Lovely Lucy,

This is the _____ of my feelings for you.
(tale)

My heart _____ when you are _____ me.
(jumps)   (near)

You are so _____ and _____ .
(pretty)   (kind)

You always make me _____ . I am here to
(grin)

_____ you from _____ . I am very
(guard)   (hurt)

_____ that you are my _____ .
(happy)   (pal)

Sincerely,
Lovesick Larry

©1998 The Education Center, Inc. • *Best Of Teacher's Helper®* • *Phonics II* • TEC931

113

Answer Key

Dear Lovely Lucy,

This is the <u>story</u> of my feelings for you.

My heart <u>leaps</u> when you are <u>beside</u> me.

You are so <u>beautiful</u> and <u>nice</u>.

You always make me <u>smile</u>. I am here to

<u>protect</u> you from <u>harm</u>. I am very <u>glad</u>

that you are my <u>friend</u>.

Sincerely,

Lovesick Larry

Name _____

The Sweet Serenade

Look at the word in each music note.
Find each word's antonym in the Word Bank.
Write the correct number on the music note.
The first one has been done for you.

Antonyms: Words that have opposite meanings.

Word Bank

1. empty
2. close
3. down
4. tall
5. cold
6. good
7. new
8. break
9. awake
10. many
11. frown
12. sloppy
13. sick
14. big

open

hot

tiny   14

few

short

bad

neat

asleep

fix

well

up

old

smile

full

Bonus Box: On the back of this sheet, illustrate a pair of antonyms from this page.

Answer Key

Petey's Polar Pops

Antonym:
Word that means the opposite.

Help Petey put his pops together.
Look at each word.
Cut and paste the antonym.

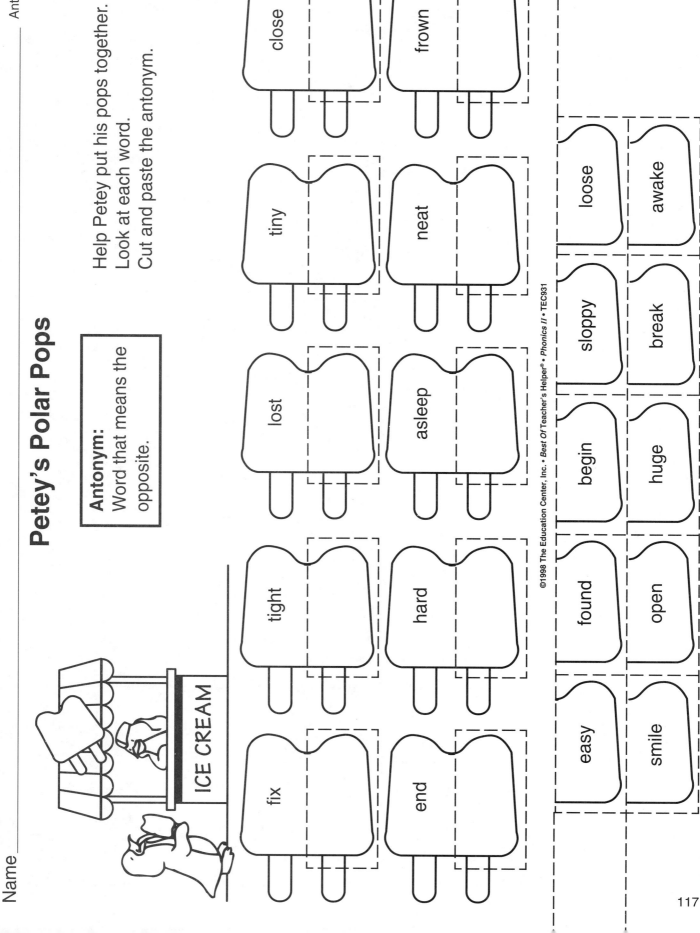

close

frown

tiny

neat

lost

asleep

tight

hard

fix

end

ICE CREAM

loose

awake

sloppy

break

begin

huge

found

open

easy

smile

©1998 The Education Center, Inc. • *Best Of Teacher's Helper®* • *Phonics II* • TEC931

Answer Key

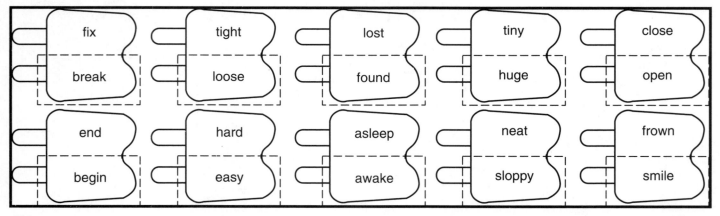

fix	tight	lost	tiny	close
break	loose	found	huge	open
end	hard	asleep	neat	frown
begin	easy	awake	sloppy	smile

Candy-Heart Confusion

Love Bug dropped his candy hearts.
Cut and glue the correct synonyms and antonyms.

Synonyms				Antonyms			
soggy		glad		cold		slow	
smile		easy		old		soft	
look		pal		weak		day	
big		lovely		float		dark	

©1998 The Education Center, Inc. • Best Of Teacher's Helper® • Phonics II • TEC931

light	simple	grin	strong	young	wet	hard

Bonus Box: Color each half of the hearts:
one-syllable words = red
two-syllable words = pink

see	happy	night	hot	pretty	sink	large	fast	buddy

Answer Key

Synonyms	Antonyms

Synonyms

soggy | wet	glad | happy
smile | grin	easy | simple
look | see	pal | buddy
big | large	lovely | pretty

Antonyms

cold | hot	slow | fast
old | young	soft | hard
weak | strong	day | night
float | sink	dark | light

Nothing Lives Alone

Read these word pairs.
Decide if they are synonyms or antonyms.
Circle the correct code letter.
Use the code letters to answer the question below.

		synonyms	antonyms				synonyms	antonyms
1.	float—sink	M	(N)	8.	little—tiny	T	S
2.	noisy—quiet	K	F	9.	dangerous—safe	A	O
3.	big—huge	H	J	10.	rude—polite	G	D
4.	finish—begin	T	R	11.	easy—difficult	U	E
5.	noisy—loud	D	C	12.	sleepy—drowsy	E	I
6.	soggy—wet	S	W	13.	cheerful—gloomy	A	O
7.	alike—same	A	E	14.	above—over	L	P

What do plants give animals?

___ ___ ___ ___   ___ ___ ___   ___ ___ ___ ___ ___ ___ ___
2 9 13 5   7 1 10   6 3 11 14 8 12 4

Label each picture **food** or **shelter** to show the plant's role.

A.

_____

B.

_____

C.

_____

D.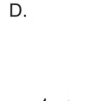

_____

E.

_____

F.

_____

Variation

Talk about plants and plant parts shown in the pictures. Discuss how birds and other animals use plants. Share kinds of plants they use.

Extension Activities

— Have students decorate a bulletin board to look like the ocean. Provide them with resource books and encyclopedias showing ocean plants (seaweed, algae, etc.). Let them cut out or draw these plants using interesting materials. Add them to the board with identifying labels.

— Pinpoint plant products used for clothing, shelter, foods, or medicines. Make a list on the blackboard as students point out objects in the room. Have students bring other items from home or pictures of products, and add these to the list. Divide the list by the four categories. Have students identify plants used to make these products, as well as parts of the plants that are used.

— Have students pretend to be plant explorers. Challenge each child to create a new plant that she has just discovered in the wild—to draw it, name it, identify the region in which it grows, and explain its uses. Let students vote on the most creative plant.

Answer Key

		synonyms	antonyms			synonyms	antonyms
1.	float—sink	M	(N)	8. little—tiny	(T)	S
2.	noisy—quiet	K	(F)	9. dangerous—safe	A	(O)
3.	big—huge	(H)	J	10. rude—polite	G	(D)
4.	finish—begin	T	(R)	11. easy—difficult	U	(E)
5.	noisy—loud	(D)	C	12. sleepy—drowsy	(E)	I
6.	soggy—wet	(S)	W	13. cheerful—gloomy	A	(O)
7.	alike—same	(A)	E	14. above—over	(L)	P

What do plants give animals?

F O O D   A N D   S H E L T E R
2 9 13 5   7 1 10   6 3 11 14 8 12 4

Label each picture **food** or **shelter** to show the plant's role.

A. shelter

B. shelter

C. food

D. food

E. shelter

F. food

Name _____

Cupid's Cuties

Color each **antonym** heart **red.**
Color each **synonym** heart **pink.**

stop
go

jog
run

pail
bucket

front
back

money
cash

lost
found

on
off

friend
pal

dark
light

top
bottom

up
down

see
look

bunny
rabbit

clean
dirty

wet
dry

Bonus Box: On the back of this sheet, draw yourself as you think you look from the back.

Variations

— White-out the directions and the words. Reprogram the page with math problems and new directions.

— White-out the directions and the words. Run the page off with blank hearts and direct students to write homonym pairs in the hearts.

Background For The Teacher
Valentine's Day

Valentine's Day, a special day for remembering sweethearts, friends, and family, was brought to America from Europe. Some people trace the origin to an ancient Roman festival called *Lupercalia,* in honor of the god Lupercus. Others believe it was named after Valentine, an early Christian imprisoned because of his refusal to worship Roman gods. He had many friends among Roman children and they tossed notes to him through the bars of his cell. Still another belief is that a Roman priest, also named Valentine, secretly married young couples against the emperor's wishes. As a result, he was executed on February 14.

The English people celebrated Valentine's Day as far back as the 1400s. That was when Charles, Duke of Orléans, sent his wife a rhymed love letter from the Tower of London where he was imprisoned. Years later, many stores sold books which included verses to copy for valentines. The first commercially produced valentines appeared in England in the 1800s. Artist Kate Greenaway became famous for her cards with pictures of happy children and beautiful gardens.

Esther A. Howland of Worcester, Massachusetts, was one of the first to produce valentines in the United States. She turned a small idea into a $100,000-a-year assembly-line business.

Extension Activities

— Use a bag of candy conversation hearts to complete several activities.
1. Count the number of pieces in the bag. Have each student write down an estimate of the number of candy pieces. Give the hearts to the winner or split them in case of a tie. Other students earn a heart sticker.
2. Separate the hearts by colors. Have students construct graphs showing the number of hearts of each color.
3. Discuss the various sayings that are on candy conversation hearts. Have each student write original sayings on several heart shapes you provide.

— Give the class an opportunity to practice creative writing by having each student write one part of a progressive story. Provide lined, heart-shaped paper to each student. Have one person start the story on his paper heart. Then pass his part to the next person who reads it and adds another part on his own paper. He then passes both paper hearts on to the next person until everyone has had a chance to add a section to the story. The last person reads all the parts and writes an ending to the story. Post on a "Hearts-to-Hearts" bulletin board.

— Have students design original valentines for classmates and friends. Use homonyms and homographs as part of the lines. For example: "My heart beets for you": have a picture of beets on the card. "I'll never tire of you": have a picture of an old, worn-out tire.

Answer Key

Name _____

Get The Scoop On Birds

Choose and write the correct prefix in each blank.

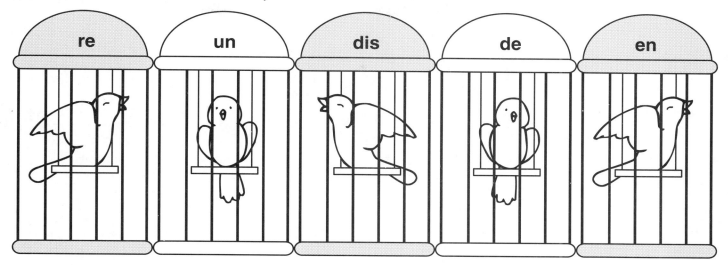

re   un   dis   de   en

1. When choosing a bird, you might consider an ____common breed.

2. If you are ____certain, ask a veterinarian to help you.

3. You will ____cover many ____usual habits of birds.

4. The shape of the cage should ____pend on the kind of bird you buy.

5. Don't forget to ____infect the cage before placing your pet inside.

6. ____place the newspaper in the bottom of the cage twice a week.

7. Your bird will be ____interested if you don't hang a mirror in the cage.

8. Most birds ____pend mainly on seeds for food.

9. You can ____ward your feathered friend with a birdseed treat.

10. ____move leftover food that would soon spoil.

11. All birds ____cover that they lose their feathers and grow new ones.

12. New feathers will be ____placed one at a time.

13. Don't ____danger your bird by leaving it in a drafty place.

14. Your new pet will ____pay you with years of ____joyment.

Bonus Box: Draw and color a pet bird on the back of this sheet. Write its name below it. Write a story about your bird.

Answer Key

1. When choosing a bird, you might consider an **un** common breed.

2. If you are **un** certain, ask a veterinarian to help you.

3. You will **dis** cover many **un** usual habits of birds.

4. The shape of the cage should **de** pend on the kind of bird you buy.

5. Don't forget to **dis** infect the cage before placing your pet inside.

6. **Re** place the newspaper in the bottom of the cage twice a week.

   dis or
7. Your bird will be **un** interested if you don't hang a mirror in the cage.

8. Most birds **de** pend mainly on seeds for food.

9. You can **re** ward your feathered friend with a birdseed treat.

10. **Re** move leftover food that would soon spoil.

11. All birds **dis** cover that they lose their feathers and grow new ones.

12. New feathers will be **re** placed one at a time.

13. Don't **en** danger your bird by leaving it in a drafty place.

14. Your new pet will **re** pay you with years of **en** joyment.

126

Suffixes: *er, est, ing, ed*

Polar Posies

Many kinds of plants grow near the North Pole.
They can live in freezing weather.
They don't grow very tall because of the strong wind.
But they have bright, beautiful flowers.

> To add *er*, *est*, *ing*, or *ed* to a word that ends in an *e*, drop the *e* and add the ending.

Write the new word on each line.

1. nice + er = _____

2. late + est = _____

3. hide + ing = _____

4. love + ed = _____

5. wide + est = _____

6. shake + ing = _____

7. brave + er = _____

8. hope + ed = _____

9. wise + est = _____

10. race + ed = _____

11. white + er = _____

12. place + ing = _____

13. save + ed = _____

14. come + ing = _____

15. amaze + ed = _____

16. fine + er = _____

Bonus Box: Pick five of the new words you wrote, and write a story about visiting the North Pole.

Variation

Have students read about kinds of plants that can live at the North Pole. Let children share when, where, and how these plants live.

Answer Key

1. nicer
2. latest
3. hiding
4. loved
5. widest
6. shaking
7. braver
8. hoped
9. wisest
10. raced
11. whiter
12. placing
13. saved
14. coming
15. amazed
16. finer

Name _____

Breakfast In Bed

Color patches with **correctly** spelled words **orange**.
Color patches with **incorrectly** spelled words **green**.

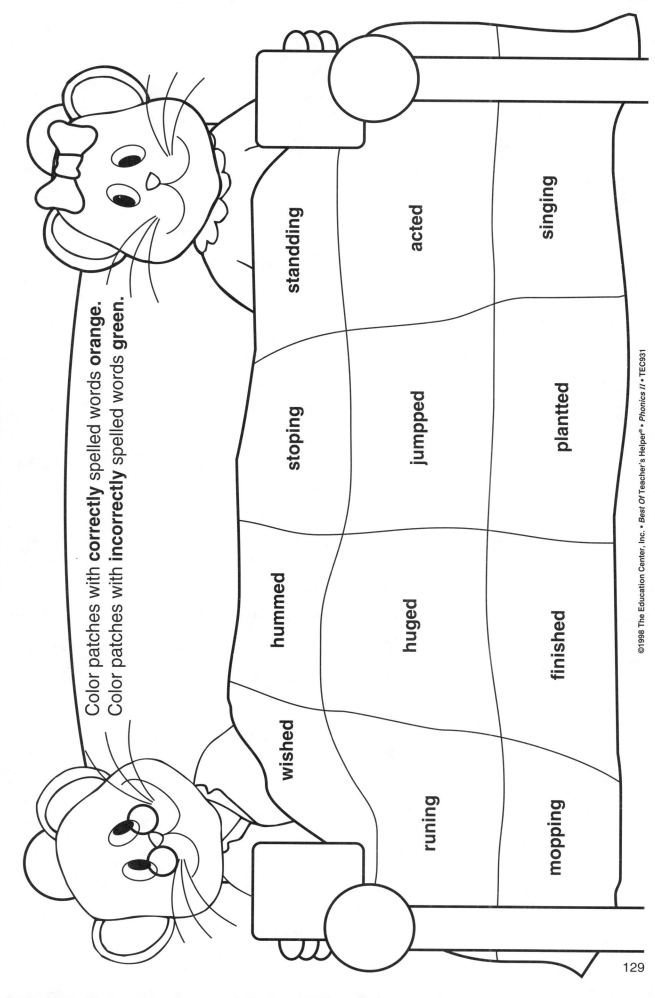

standding	stoping	hummed
		wished
acted	jumpped	huged
		runing
singing	plantted	finished
		mopping

Answer Key

wished
orange

hummed
orange

stoping
green

standding
green

runing
green

huged
green

jumpped
green

acted
orange

mopping
orange

finished
orange

plantted
green

singing
orange

Bags Of Booty

Add *ing* and *ed* to each word.
Write the new words on the lines.
Color the jewels.

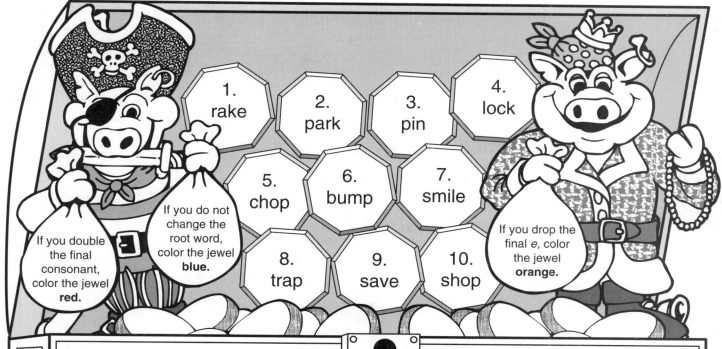

1. rake
2. park
3. pin
4. lock
5. chop
6. bump
7. smile
8. trap
9. save
10. shop

If you double the final consonant, color the jewel **red.**

If you do not change the root word, color the jewel **blue.**

If you drop the final *e*, color the jewel **orange.**

ed	ing
1. _____	_____
2. _____	_____
3. _____	_____
4. _____	_____
5. _____	_____
6. _____	_____
7. _____	_____
8. _____	_____
9. _____	_____
10. _____	_____

Answer Key

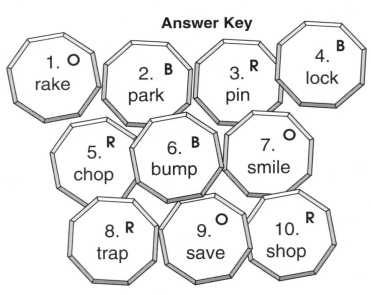

1. O rake
2. B park
3. R pin
4. B lock
5. R chop
6. B bump
7. O smile
8. R trap
9. O save
10. R shop

1. raked	raking
2. parked	parking
3. pinned	pinning
4. locked	locking
5. chopped	chopping
6. bumped	bumping
7. smiled	smiling
8. trapped	trapping
9. saved	saving
10. shopped	shopping

Slam Dunk!

Add the suffix *er* to each base word.
Write the new word under the play you used.

Base Words

walk	bank	write
bat	shop	skate
close	bake	hunt
drive	dig	
sing	call	
win	drum	

One-Point Play
Add the suffix without changing the base word.

Two-Point Play
Drop the final *e* before adding the suffix.

Three-Point Play
Double the final consonant before adding the suffix.

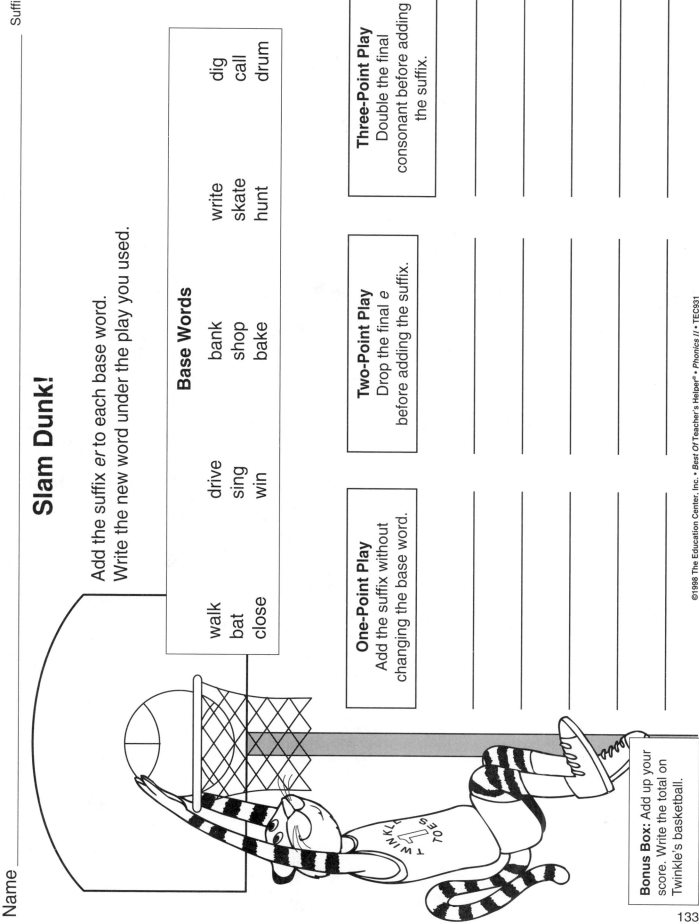

Bonus Box: Add up your score. Write the total on Twinkle's basketball.

Variation

This activity requires only a minimal amount of reprogramming to provide practice adding the suffix *ing* to base words. In the directions simply white-out the suffix *er* and reprogram with the suffix *ing*.

Paper Topper

Duplicate copies of the paper-topper pattern on white construction paper. Color and laminate them; then cut them out. Use the paper toppers to enhance student work such as the suffix project described on page 140.

Pattern

©1998 The Education Center, Inc. • *Best Of Teacher's Helper® • Phonics II* • TEC931

Answer Key
(Order of answers will vary.)

One-Point Play	Two-Point Play	Three-Point Play
walker	closer	batter
singer	driver	winner
banker	baker	shopper
hunter	writer	digger
caller	skater	drummer

Bonus Box answer: 30

Name _____

Going For The Goal!

Make new words by adding the suffix *less* or *ness* to each base word.
Write each word under the correct suffix.

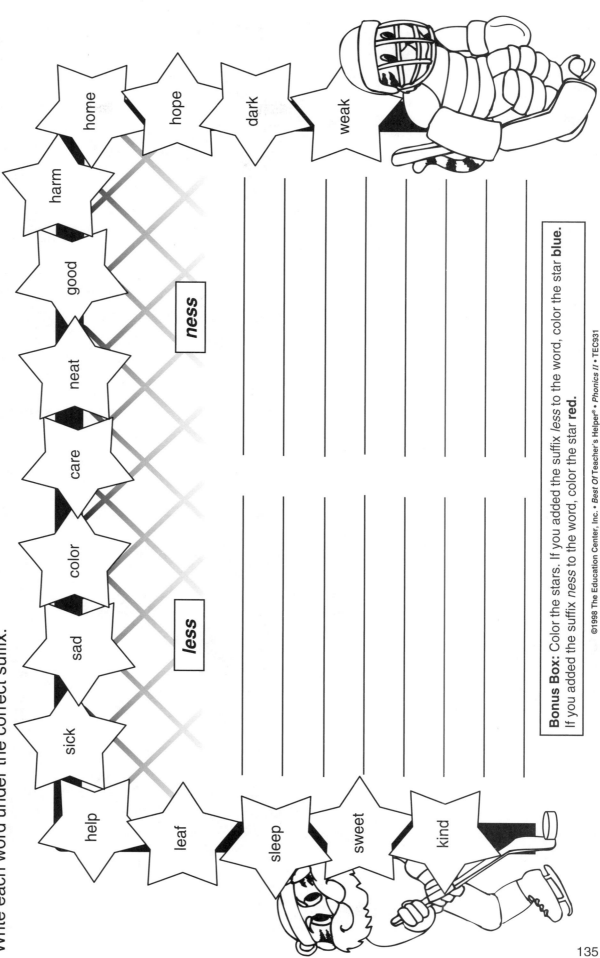

home
hope
dark
weak
harm
good
neat
care
color
sad
sick
help
leaf
sleep
sweet
kind

ness

less

Bonus Box: Color the stars. If you added the suffix *less* to the word, color the star **blue.**
If you added the suffix *ness* to the word, color the star **red.**

©1998 The Education Center, Inc. • *Best Of Teacher's Helper® • Phonics II* • TEC931

135

Variations

— White-out and reprogram a copy of the activity to reinforce additional suffix pairs. For example, after reprogramming the directions to instruct students to add the suffixes *able* and *en* to the base words, program the stars as follows: read, sick, weak, laugh, short, wear, clean, fresh, agree, dark, drink, sweet, hard, train, maid, enjoy. (Be sure to adjust the suffix headings and Bonus Box to match.)

— Or—after whiting-out the programming on a copy of the activity—reprogram the directions to instruct students to add the suffixes *er* and *est* to each word. Program the suffix headings; then program only eight stars. The following base words can be used: small, slow, happy, hungry, fast, sleepy, angry, hot. Be sure to remind students that when a word ends in *y*, they need to change the *y* to *i* before adding a suffix. Also remind them that C-V-C words need to have the last consonant doubled before a suffix. (If desired, the Bonus Box activity may read, "Color the stars.")

Answer Key

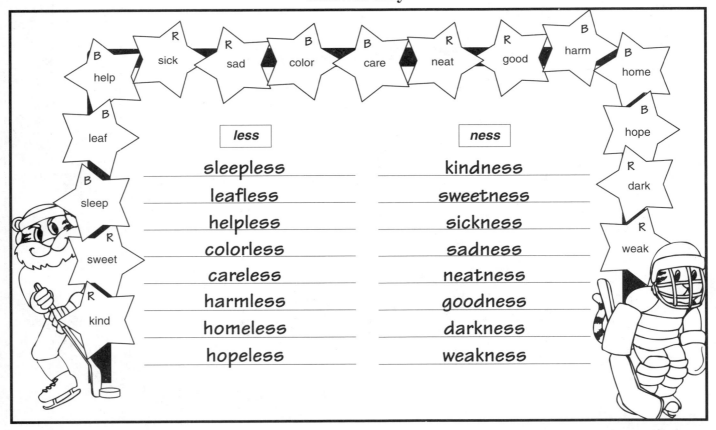

less	ness
sleepless	kindness
leafless	sweetness
helpless	sickness
colorless	sadness
careless	neatness
harmless	goodness
homeless	darkness
hopeless	weakness

Name _____

Cub Cards

Each member of the Cubs football team has a nickname.
Read the clue at the bottom of each card.
Complete each player's nickname.
The first one is done for you.

Remember to capitalize the first letter of each name!

___Hope___**ful Hank**

Hank always hopes
his team will win.

_____**ful Conrad**

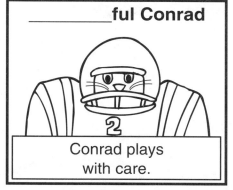

Conrad plays
with care.

_____**ful Harry**

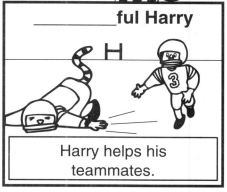

Harry helps his
teammates.

_____**ful Sam**

Sam is a very
skilled player.

_____**ful Jed**

Jed is full
of joy.

_____**ful Willie**

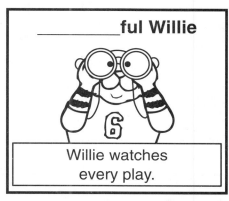

Willie watches
every play.

_____**ful Clyde**

Clyde likes
bright colors.

_____**ful Calvin**

Calvin cheers up
his teammates.

_____**ful Pete**

Pete loves to
play tricks.

_____**ful Felix**

Felix forgets
everything!

_____**ful Patrick**

Patrick is full of
power.

_____**ful Wally**

Wally wishes he
could score.

Follow-Up Activities

— Transform the pattern below into booklets. To do so, duplicate two construction-paper copies of the pattern for each student. After students have cut out and personalized the patterns as desired, have them staple several blank pages (traced from and cut into the patterns' shape) between the resulting covers. Students can write football stories, facts, or biographies about the players featured on the Cub cards in their booklets.

— Have students color and cut out their completed cards, then glue the cards in alphabetical order on a sheet of construction paper.

Pattern

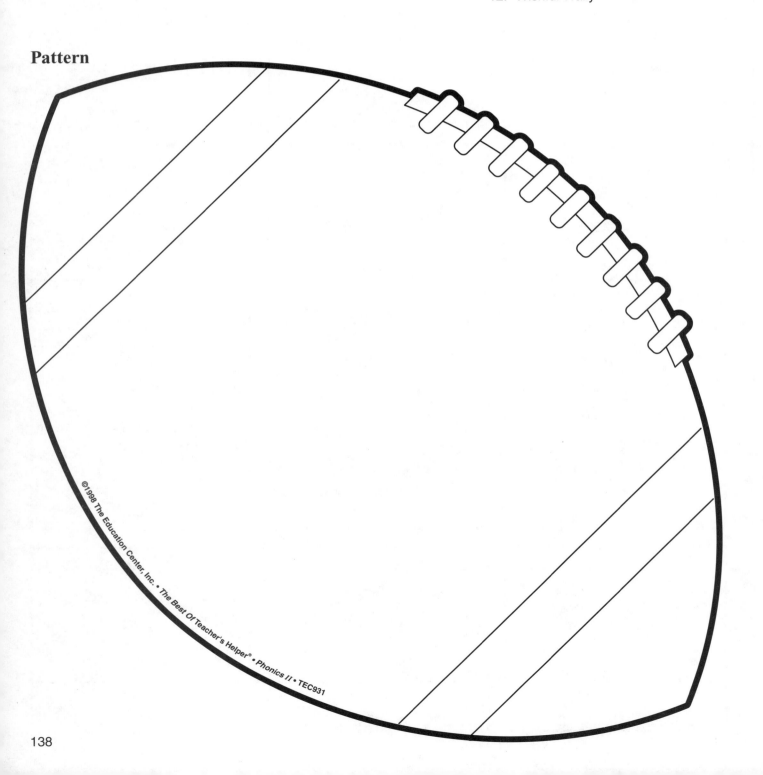

©1998 The Education Center, Inc. • The Best Of Teacher's Helper® • Phonics II • TEC931

Batter Up!

Add the suffix *ly* to each base word below.
Cut and paste to complete each sentence.

1. It was a _____ day at Tiger Stadium.

2. The sun shone _____ .

3. The fans _____ found their seats.

4. The game started _____ at noon.

5. The umpire seemed very _____ .

6. The fans watched the game very _____ .

7. _____ the game was tied!

8. The crowd cheered _____ .

9. Both teams _____ wanted to score.

10. _____ the last batter stepped up to the plate.

11. The batter _____ even swung the bat.

12. But the ball _____ sailed out of the park!

| Sudden____ | love____ | Final____ | bright____ | real____ | exact____ |
| quick____ | hard____ | friend____ | loud____ | close____ | near____ |

Extension Activity
Sports/Suffixes

This sporty suffix activity is sure to be a hit with your youngsters. And later (if desired) the completed projects can be used as learning center activities. To begin, ask students to cut a predetermined number of words with suffixes from discarded magazines and/or newspapers. You may want to have each student personalize a business-size envelope and store his word collection inside.

Enlist an adult volunteer to help each student cut the shape of a piece of sports equipment (such as an ice-hockey stick or puck, a football or football helmet, a basketball, or a baseball or baseball bat) from a fairly large piece of bulletin-board paper. After students have personalized and added desired details to their cutouts, have them glue their word collections on the shapes. Next have each child sequentially number the words on his cutout, then make an answer key for his project on another sheet of paper. The answer key should indicate the suffixes that were added to the base words featured on the student's cutout. Have each student glue his completed answer key to the back of his cutout.

Attach a paper topper to each cutout (see page 134) and display the projects around the classroom. Or display the projects a few at a time in a learning center. To complete the center, a student chooses a cutout and then writes on his numbered paper the suffix added to each base word. He then flips the cutout over to check his work.

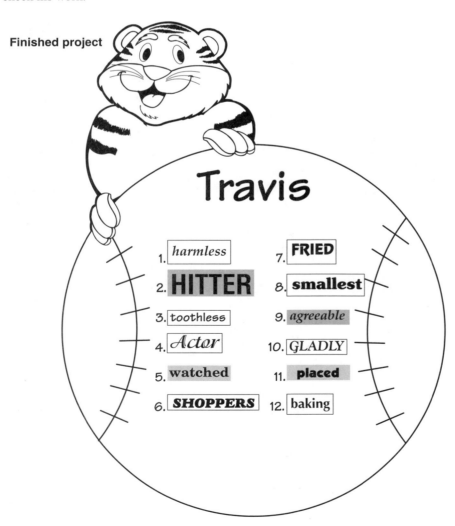

Finished project

Travis

1. *harmless* 7. **FRIED**
2. **HITTER** 8. **smallest**
3. toothless 9. *agreeable*
4. *Actor* 10. GLADLY
5. **watched** 11. **placed**
6. **SHOPPERS** 12. baking

Red Knight Racer

Plural means more than one.
Look at each word.
Write the plural form on the line.

box
_____

star
_____

key
_____

Add *s* to most words
to make them plural.

glass
_____

inch
_____

tree
_____

church
_____

book
_____

Add *es* to words ending
with *ss, x, z, ch,* and *sh.*

girl
_____

buzz
_____

ax
_____

chair
_____

Bonus Box: Find examples of plurals in the classroom. Make a list on the back of this sheet.

Background For The Teacher
Race Cars

Auto racing, which started in the 1890s, entertains millions of people worldwide each year. Despite the variations within the sport, all auto races have one common denominator—the high risk of imminent danger.

The pursuit of that thrill spawned an enormous number of events. The different kinds of races can be categorized as follows: (1) stock car racing, (2) drag racing, (3) sports car racing, (4) Formula One racing, and (5) Indy car racing. These races are classified according to the type of car and track used.

Stock car racing, the most popular auto racing in the United States, started in the South. Only American-made production cars (factory-made cars that have been changed for racing) are allowed. Most stock car races take place on oval asphalt tracks that measure anywhere from 1/5 mile to 2 2/3 miles. The Daytona 500 is an example of stock car racing.

Extension Activities

— Give each student a piece of white construction paper and crayons. As a class, brainstorm a list of plurals. Have each student choose one plural word from the list to illustrate. Have students label their pictures with the plural words. Sandwich student work between colorful construction paper, punch holes, and tie it together with colorful ribbon or yarn lengths. Entitle the book "Our Book Of Plurals" and place it in the reading corner for students to enjoy during individual reading time.

— Extend your plurals unit with a plurals race! Divide the class into two teams. To play, state a plural rule. A student from team one must give an example word for the rule. If correct, that team receives a point. If incorrect, no point is given and a player from the opposing team is given a chance to score. Then state a new rule for team two and continue play as before. Have students on each team take turns and continue play until all students have had a chance to play.

— For this activity, have each student bring an old newspaper from home. Have student pairs circle as many plural words as they can find in a predetermined amount of time. Then, as a class, have students share their plural findings. Award the student pair finding the most plurals with a healthful snack such as raisins or nuts (in plural form, of course).

Answer Key

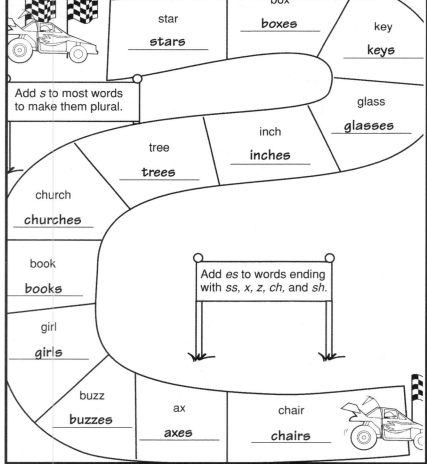

Name _____

An Ice-Cream Dream

Write the plural of each word on the line below it.
Use the hint below to help you.

12. bug
_____

13. bunch
_____

Chocolate Swirl

10. star
_____

11. wish
_____

7. apple
_____

8. peach
_____

9. dish
_____

4. box
_____

5. buzz
_____

6. fox
_____

1. dress
_____

2. ball
_____

3. beach
_____

Vanilla Berry

Hint:

Add *es* to words ending
in *x*, *ss*, *zz*, *sh*, and *ch*.

Bonus Box: Make up three new flavors of ice cream. On the back of this sheet, write the name of each flavor and its ingredients.

©1998 The Education Center, Inc. • *Best Of Teacher's Helper® • Phonics II* • TEC931

143

Background For The Teacher
Ice Cream

The main ingredients in ice cream are milk, cream, eggs, sugar, vanilla, and a small amount of salt. To make ice cream, the milk and cream are heated together. The eggs and sugar are added next. This mixture is heated to an extremely high temperature to kill germs. The mixture is then put into a machine called a *homogenizer*. This machine makes the ice cream smooth. Salt is added next and then the mixture is cooled. After it cools for a while, vanilla or other flavorings are added. Then the mixture is cooled down for several hours. Finally the mixture is cooled even more and then is quickly frozen. After the final freezing, the mixture has become ice cream. Other ingredients—such as nuts, candy, and fruit—can be added at this time.

How would you like to have a job as a professional ice-cream tester? When judging ice cream, professional ice-cream testers check for many things. They check to see if the color looks nice and if the color matches the flavor. They also check to see how quickly the ice cream melts. Professionals say that the best ice cream melts quickly at room temperature. Ice-cream testers look for ice cream that drips easily and feels smooth and creamy in the mouth.

Follow-Up Activity
Easy Ice Cream

Your class will love this tasty version of homemade ice cream. It's easy to make and you won't even need to use an ice-cream maker! To make a small batch of ice cream, you need the following ingredients:

    1 cup sugar
    1/2 cup milk
    1/2 cup cream
    1 tablespoon vanilla

Combine the ingredients in a bowl and let the mixture stand for a few minutes. Place the mixture in the freezer until it is partially frozen (approximately five hours). Remove the bowl from the freezer and beat the mixture until it is stiff. Freeze the mixture overnight. For a class of 30 students, this recipe makes enough ice cream for each child to have a spoonful.

Answer Key

1. dresses
2. balls
3. beaches

4. boxes
5. buzzes
6. foxes

7. apples
8. peaches
9. dishes

10. stars
11. wishes

12. bugs
13. bunches

Polar Plurals

Read the Plural Tips.
Fill in the plural ending for each word.
Write the plural word on the line.

Plural Tips
To make most nouns plural, **add s.**
If a noun ends in *ss, x, ch, zz,* or *sh,* **add es.**
If a noun ends in *y,* **change the *y* to *i* and add *es*.**

1. seal + (s) (es) (ies) = _____

2. party + (s) (es) (ies) = _____

3. bush + (s) (es) (ies) = _____

4. cherry + (s) (es) (ies) = _____

5. egg + (s) (es) (ies) = _____

6. peach + (s) (es) (ies) = _____

7. whale + (s) (es) (ies) = _____

8. cross + (s) (es) (ies) = _____

9. berry + (s) (es) (ies) = _____

10. bear + (s) (es) (ies) = _____

11. baby + (s) (es) (ies) = _____

12. family + (s) (es) (ies) = _____

13. box + (s) (es) (ies) = _____

14. ocean + (s) (es) (ies) = _____

15. lady + (s) (es) (ies) = _____

1.	seal	+	(s)	(es)	(ies)	=	seals
2.	party	+	(s)	(es)	(ies)	=	parties
3.	bush	+	(s)	(es)	(ies)	=	bushes
4.	cherry	+	(s)	(es)	(ies)	=	cherries
5.	egg	+	(s)	(es)	(ies)	=	eggs
6.	peach	+	(s)	(es)	(ies)	=	peaches
7.	whale	+	(s)	(es)	(ies)	=	whales
8.	cross	+	(s)	(es)	(ies)	=	crosses
9.	berry	+	(s)	(es)	(ies)	=	berries
10.	bear	+	(s)	(es)	(ies)	=	bears
11.	baby	+	(s)	(es)	(ies)	=	babies
12.	family	+	(s)	(es)	(ies)	=	families
13.	box	+	(s)	(es)	(ies)	=	boxes
14.	ocean	+	(s)	(es)	(ies)	=	oceans
15.	lady	+	(s)	(es)	(ies)	=	ladies

Name _____

Puppy Love

Read each word.
Write its plural on the heart.
Color the hearts using the code.

glass
_____

peach
_____

berry
_____

spider
_____

chair
_____

baby
_____

spoon
_____

city
_____

fox
_____

shoe
_____

brush
_____

bus
_____

party
_____

pencil
_____

puppy
_____

Color Code

Add **s** = Color red

Add **es** = Color purple

Change **y** to **i**
and add **es** = Color pink

Plural Pointers

Read the plural rules on the penguins' signs.
Decide which plural rule to use.
Draw the symbol on the line.
Use the symbols on the signs.

To make most nouns plural, **add s**.

If a noun ends in *ss, x, ch, zz,* or *sh*, **add es**.

If a noun ends in *y*, **change the y to i and add es.**

1. winter _____

2. ocean _____

3. city _____

4. bush _____

5. family _____

6. compass _____

7. cross _____

8. boot _____

9. berry _____

10. lady _____

11. fox _____

12. seal _____

Rewrite the words in their plural forms.

1. _____

2. _____

3. _____

4. _____

5. _____

6. _____

7. _____

8. _____

9. _____

10. _____

11. _____

12. _____

Bonus Box: Choose one *s* plural word, one *es* plural word, and one *ies* plural word from above. On the back of this sheet, use each word in a sentence.

Award

Duplicate this award for students who have earned outstanding noun scores, have completed the noun unit, or have shown progress with their noun skills.

The Noun Pole

Explorer's name

has successfully reached

the Noun Pole!

Congratulations!

Noun expedition supervisor

Answer Key

1. winter ●	2. ocean ●	3. city ■
4. bush ▲	5. family ■	6. compass ▲
7. cross ▲	8. boot ●	9. berry ■
10. lady ■	11. fox ▲	12. seal ●

1. winters	2. oceans	3. cities
4. bushes	5. families	6. compasses
7. crosses	8. boots	9. berries
10. ladies	11. foxes	12. seals

Name _____

Blue Challenger Change

Look at the words.
Circle the nouns that end with a consonant and **y.**
Write the plural form of the circled words on the blanks.

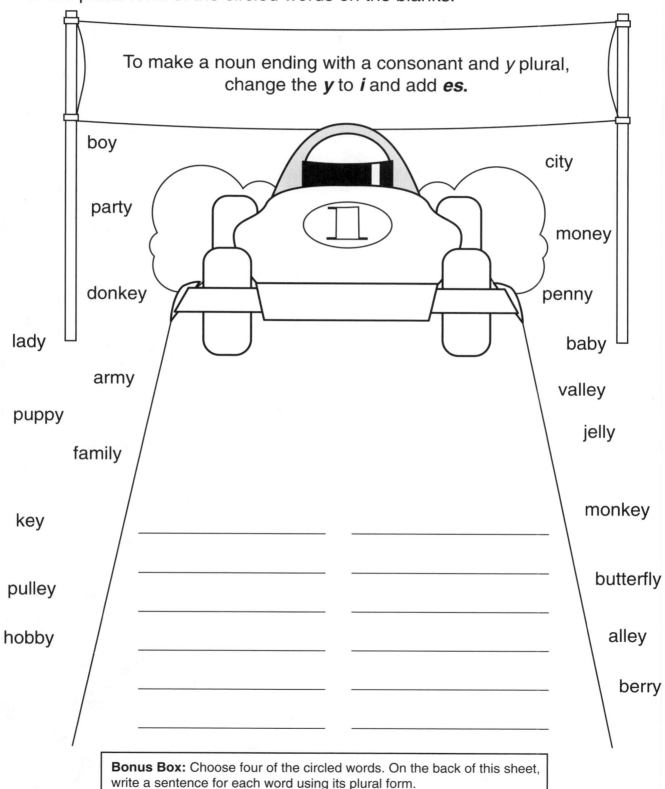

To make a noun ending with a consonant and *y* plural,
change the **y** to **i** and add **es.**

boy

party

donkey

lady

army

puppy

family

key

pulley

hobby

city

money

penny

baby

valley

jelly

monkey

butterfly

alley

berry

Bonus Box: Choose four of the circled words. On the back of this sheet, write a sentence for each word using its plural form.

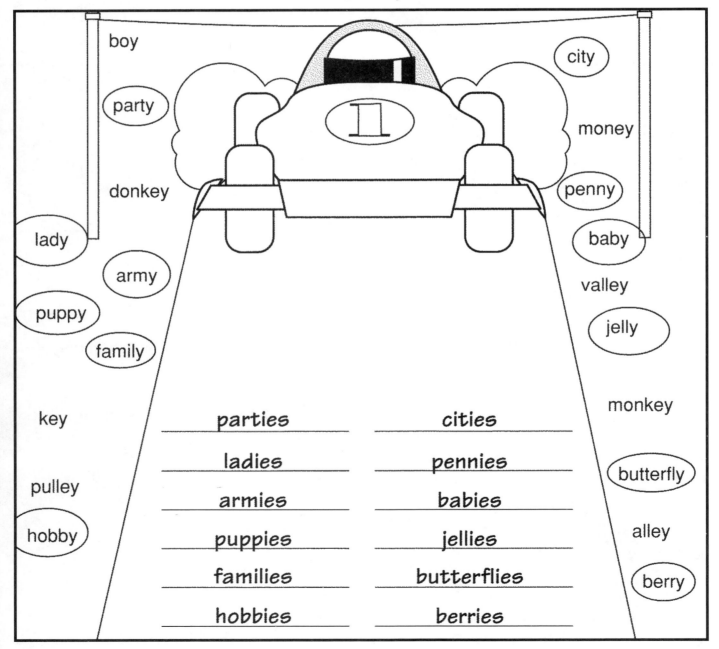

boy

party

donkey

lady

army

puppy

family

city

money

penny

baby

valley

jelly

monkey

butterfly

alley

berry

key

pulley

hobby

parties	cities
ladies	pennies
armies	babies
puppies	jellies
families	butterflies
hobbies	berries

Name_____

I Scream For Ice Cream

Look at the words on the ice-cream truck.
Circle each word that ends with a consonant and *y*.
Write the plural of each word in the correct column.

Hints:
If a word ends in a consonant and *y*,
change the *y* to *i* and add *es*.
If a word ends in a vowel and *y*,
just add *s*.

belly	berry	guppy
day	alley	cherry
puppy	jelly	boy
toy		tray valley

Change *y* to *i* and add *es*.

Just add *s*.

_____

_____

_____

_____

_____

_____

Bonus Box: Each word above rhymes with another word. On the back of this sheet, write each pair of rhyming words.

How To Use This Bookmark

Duplicate the bookmark below on construction paper for each of your students. Have each child color the ice-cream cone and then cut out the bookmark. Then have each child cut on the dotted line on his bookmark. (Students may need assistance with this step.) To use the bookmark, the child hooks the cut section of the bookmark over a page as shown.

Bookmark

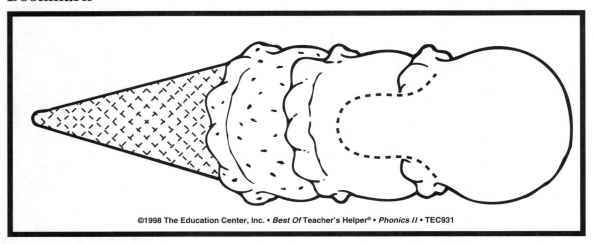

Example

Answer Key

Change *y* to *i* and add *es.*	Just add *s.*	Bonus Box:
bellies	days	bellies, jellies
puppies	toys	puppies, guppies
berries	alleys	berries, cherries
jellies	trays	days, trays
guppies	valleys	toys, boys
cherries	boys	alleys, valleys

Name _____

Pit Stop Review

Look at each word.
Cut and paste to make each word plural.

Add **s** to most words to make them plural.

Add **es** to words ending with *ss, x, z, ch,* and *sh.*

To make a noun ending with a consonant and *y* plural, change the **y** to **i** and add **es.**

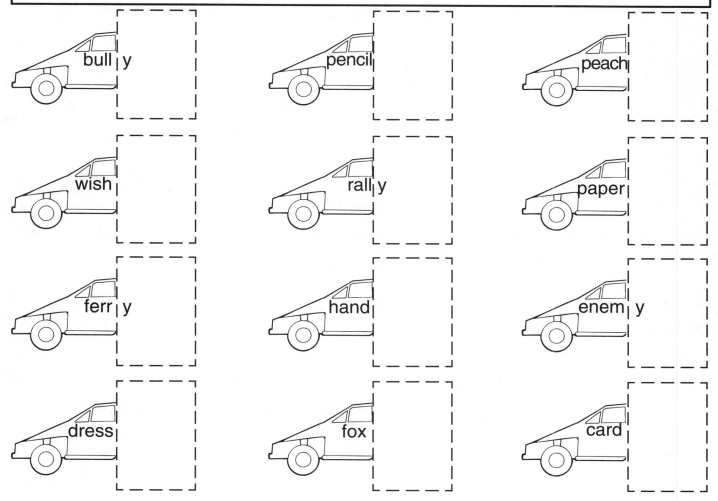

bull y	pencil	peach
wish	rall y	paper
ferr y	hand	enem y
dress	fox	card

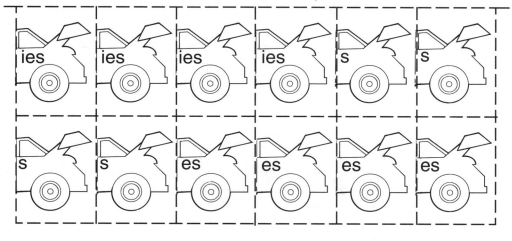

ies ies ies ies s s

s s es es es es

155

Answer Key

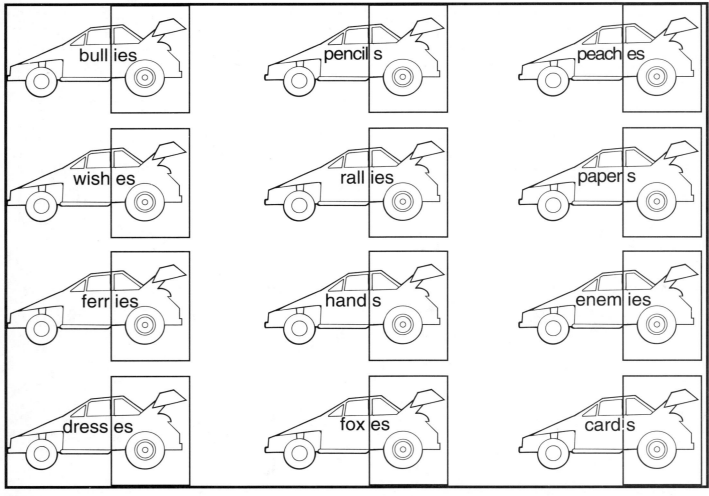

bull|ies   pencil|s   peach|es

wish|es   rall|ies   paper|s

ferr|ies   hand|s   enem|ies

dress|es   fox|es   card|s

Name_____

Ice-Cream Teams

Look at each team's shirts.
Look at the words in the Word Bank.
Write the plural of each word ending in *f* or *fe* in the box below the correct team.

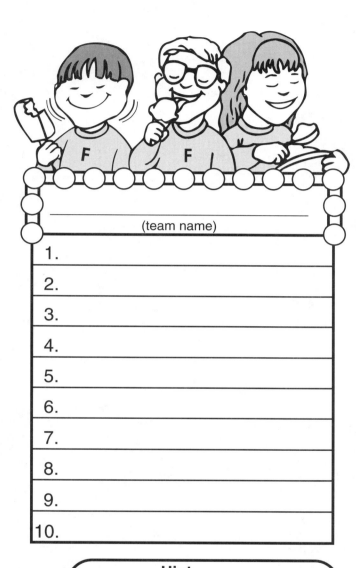

_____
(team name)

1.
2.
3.
4.
5.
6.
7.
8.
9.
10.

_____
(team name)

1.
2.
3.
4.
5.
6.
7.
8.
9.
10.

Hint
Change the *f* or *fe* to *v* before adding *es*.

❄ Mr. Freezie ❄

Word Bank

calf	wolf	scarf
wife	shelf	half
elf	life	hoof
knife	thief	leaf
	loaf	

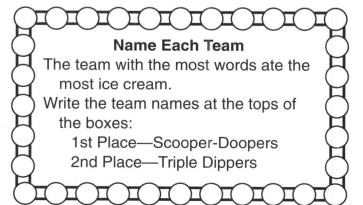

Name Each Team
The team with the most words ate the most ice cream.
Write the team names at the tops of the boxes:
   1st Place—Scooper-Doopers
   2nd Place—Triple Dippers

Answer Key

(Order of answers may vary.)

Scooper Doopers (first place)

1. calves
2. elves
3. wolves
4. shelves
5. thieves
6. scarves
7. halves
8. hooves
9. leaves
10. loaves

Triple Dippers (second place)

1. wives
2. knives
3. lives

"Bearly" Believable

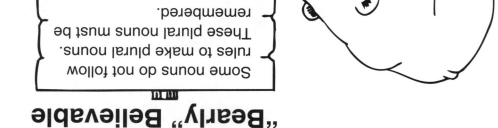

Some nouns do not follow rules to make plural nouns. These plural nouns must be remembered.

one fish

two fish

Draw a line from each noun to its plural.

child	deer	women	sheep
woman	feet	sheep	deer
foot	children	tooth	foot
deer	sheep	mouse	woman
mice	goose	man	fish
fish	man	geese	child
men	mouse	tooth	deer
teeth	fish	women	sheep

Cover the nouns above.
For each noun below, write the plural noun in the puzzle.
Uncover the nouns to check your answers.

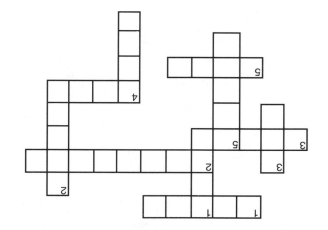

Across

1. woman
2. child
3. goose
4. fish
5. deer

Down

1. mouse
2. tooth
3. man
4. foot
5. sheep

Bonus Box: Turn your sheet over. List as many of the nouns and their plurals from this page as you can. Write a sentence telling what you learned on this page. How well did you remember?

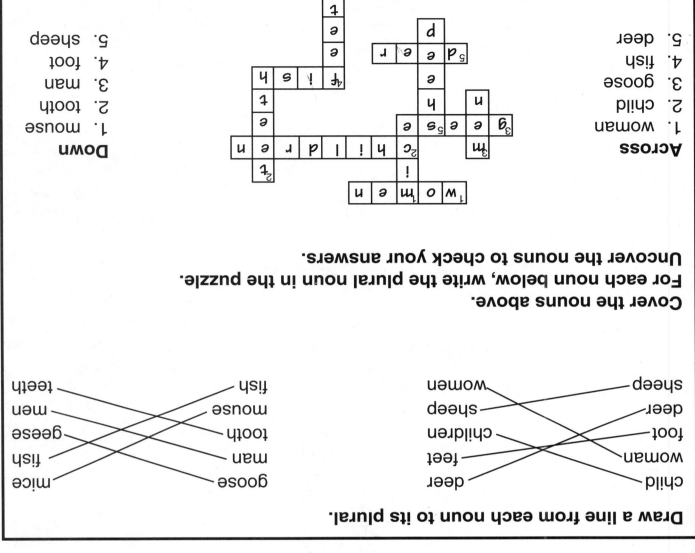

Answer Key

Draw a line from each noun to its plural.

child — deer
woman — feet
foot — children
deer — sheep
sheep — women

fish — goose
mouse — man
tooth — fish
man — geese
goose — mice

Cover the nouns above.
For each noun below, write the plural noun in the puzzle.
Uncover the nouns to check your answers.

Across
1. woman
2. child
3. goose
4. fish
5. deer

Down
1. mouse
2. tooth
3. man
4. foot
5. sheep